Raising a Strong-Willed Child

Parenting Children Who Live By Their Own Rules Without Losing Your Mind

Grace Cohen

Contents

Bonus Ebooks (Scan QR Code Below)

https://gracecohenbooks.com

Introduction

Sammy has just turned three and is quite a talker. He is a very curious kid and he can easily pick up whatever new words his family would teach him. Lately, he has been fascinated with a new word, using it at every occasion. He seems fixated with this word to the irritation of his parents.

"Mommy, I want to watch 'The Three Bears Show,' NOW!" Sammy yelled at his mother.

"Sweetie, you can't. You are only allowed one hour of video time every day and you've used it all up. Tomorrow, you can watch one episode."

"But I want it NOW. Not tomorrow, but NOW," Sammy bellowed.

"Well, you can't. And that's the end of it," Marcia was tensing up. She was beginning to regret teaching the word 'now' to little Sammy. And now, she just didn't know what to do whenever he seemed so adamant in getting his way.

"Go to your dad or play with your toys. Mommy is busy at the moment. Can you do that for me, please?" Marcia pleaded. She had a thousand things to do this morning, and Sammy's TV show was the least of her worries. And with his whining, she can't seem to focus on sorting the clothes for the laundry.

"No. I want to watch 'The Three Bears Show' NOW." He started kicking things around. Sammy thrashed the chairs around, knocking some of them over. He threw his toys at Marcia and collapsed on the floor, crying and flailing his arms around. "Now, now, now, I want to watch right now."

The noise Sammy made was getting on Marcia's nerves. It had been a peaceful morning until the TV show topic came up. And now, the house was all a mess. Marcia's head was throbbing from all the noise and kicking Sammy was making. She wanted to shout right back at Sammy and drown his yelling with her snarls. She thought of spanking him to give him a lesson. Just once would do the trick. After much thought, she changed her mind. She didn't want to be that mom who'd wallop her kids so she could have his way.

And with a resigned tone, Marcia said "All right, calm down. Stop thrashing about, it's just a TV show. I'll let you off this time, but that means you won't have your one hour of TV time tomorrow. Honey, is this a deal?"

Sammy stopped his ruckus and thought for a moment. "Yes, mommy. I want to watch 'The Three Bears' now." He hurriedly propped himself in the living room in front of the television.

Marcia turned on the TV and the house returned to its normal peace. After just a few minutes, Sammy could be heard squealing with delight as he happily watched his favorite characters.

She returned to her chores for the day, facing up to the many tasks needed to be done. From the corner of her eye, she could see little Sammy bouncing up and down as he danced to the songs from the TV program.

"He's a good kid," Marcia thought to herself. But she couldn't help but feel bad for herself.

"I'm such a pushover," she thought as she rummaged through the laundry. For sure, little Sammy would have a fit tomorrow when he wouldn't be able to watch his favorite TV show. He may be a cooperative kid, but tomorrow, he would have forgotten their little promise.

Marcia knew she would give in every time Sammy had his tantrums. She abhorred the noise but she hated upsetting her kid. An overwhelming sense of helplessness washed over her as she marched off to the laundry.

Have you ever thought that your child was somehow more stubborn, more self-independent, or more obstinate than others? Does every request to them become a constant pleading or a tug-of-war? Are you tired of always haggling for your child to obey you, always getting refused by your indignant child? Well, you are not alone.

Children come in all shapes and sizes, but all of them are gifts nonetheless. Some kids are just more obedient than others. Some kids are rather tough to deal with. We never know which one we'll get. But beyond looking at their different quirks, we have to appreciate the blessings our children are. No matter how difficult they may sometimes be, our children are our greatest source of joy and fulfillment. Given that, there are just some children who are strong-willed

I have come across several families who would come up to me for advice regarding their child. I have neighbors complaining about how they can't make their child fix the bed or wash the dishes. Some come up to me sharing their stories of haggling with their children to stop throwing a tantrum in public. And more and more, I am convinced that most families harbor one or two strong-willed children that can rather be harder to care for than most children.

And so this book was borne out of that desire to capture those vivid experiences of struggle most parents have with their strong-willed children. I have seen how parents struggle in understanding and caring for them. My heart goes out to all those parents who seem lost and clueless on the best way to raise their willful child. But my heart goes out even more to these strong-willed children who are simply wanting to be recognized and to be guided. I believe that these negative exaggerations of willful behavior simply mask the real child just wanting to be loved and understood.

This is not a comfortable book. If you think that this book is about how you can change your children to make them do your will, then you have landed on the wrong book. Our children are not puppets we can control and bend to our own will. They have their own will which we can only guide and nourish. Unless we appreciate our children as persons unique and different from us, our efforts to make them carbon copies of ourselves will remain futile.

Likewise, this book is not a guidebook to change your children. Rather, it will help you change your perspective about yourself and your child. The change should first come from you as the parent and your children will simply blossom. When we open ourselves to change, then we will be in a better position to influence our children to pursue their fullest potential. If you are convinced that every child is lovable and capable of loving in their unique ways, then this book is for you. Let me be your guide into this transformational journey for you and your family.

Chapter 1

Is My Child Too Strong-Willed?

"Emma, can you please pick up your dolls and place them in the right box?" Amelia was having a field day, doing her weekly general cleaning. She had just finished with the kitchen and the living room. As she moved to the children's bedrooms, she couldn't help but be disappointed. She had told her four-year-old Emma to organize her things an hour ago, but her dolls were still scattered all over the floor."

"Mommy, I'm busy." Emma was not to be disturbed apparently, as she was scribbling through her drawing pad. She seemed intent on finishing her masterpiece of drawing their house that she forgot about her chores.

"I'm sure that's a nice drawing you have there. But didn't I tell you that you can only use your drawing materials if you have placed your other toys in the right boxes?" Amelia was starting to raise her voice.

"In fifteen minutes Mom, I will be finished. Just give me some more time." Emma said in between strokes of her crayons.

"No. I have given you an hour already. You always keep putting off your work, asking for more time. But I won't allow it this time. Emma, I'm telling you to place your doll back where they belong." Amelia half-shouted.

"No. I will do it after I'm finished with this drawing." Emma insisted. Her strokes were more violent now as she tried to contain her anger.

"If you don't clean up your dolls, I will put them in the trash bag. I will give them to other kids who will take care of them better. And we will never buy dolls for you anymore. You keep breaking them anyway. Do you understand what I am saying?" Amelia was already at the top of her voice. There were other rooms she still had to clean and she resented the idea of being held up from her cleaning duty by her uncooperative daughter.

"No! You can't throw my dolls out! I will clean my room after I finish my drawing." Emma pleaded for the last time.

"That's the last straw for me." And with that, Amelia took her daughter's dolls and shoved them into the trash bag. She stomped off to the next room, ignorant of her daughter's sobbing and wailing.

"You are always testing me Emma. I told you many times already to clean up your toys. And this is what you get for being stubborn. I won't buy new dolls for you no matter how much you cry or thrash about."

The rest of the morning went by with Emma wailing the whole day, asking for her dolls. But Amelia was determined to make her point. If she softened and returned her daughter's dolls now, then she wouldn't be teaching Emma who was in charge. Amelia felt guilty for throwing out her daughter's beloved toys. But she also felt that it was a teaching moment she needed to make. She just turned on the vacuum cleaner so she didn't have to hear Emma's pitiful cries as she resumed cleaning the house.

"She'll get over it," Amelia thought to herself.

If you were asked to describe your child's dominant behavior, what would you say? Being strong-willed captures a range of adjectives and descriptions. Take a moment now and try to find words that could best capture your child's temperament or attitude.

Do these words describe your child?

- Stubborn

- Bossy

- Difficult to be with

- Whiny

- Determined to always do things his own way

- Impatient

- Says 'No' all the time

- Throws tantrums easily

- Refuses to compromise

- Self-independent

- Learns by himself

- Makes definite decisions

- Has set ways of doing things

- Inflexible to changes

- Resolute

- Accomplishes tasks to the end

- Passionate about an activity

- Energetic

As you can see in this selection, being strong-willed is a mix of both positive and negative attributes. You might be reading this book because you assessed that your child may have a behavioral problem. This is only partly true. Before we can completely label them as 'misbehaving,' we have to appreciate how willfulness can also be a gift your child could have.

The Gift of Being Strong-Willed

It might be difficult to appreciate strong willfulness as a gift when your kid is having a fit of tantrums or refusing to obey your commands. It's easier to dismiss all these attitudes as defiant or even destructive behavior altogether. Because we don't understand them, we simply describe their behavior as 'bad' or 'inappropriate.' But if you start on the notion that being willful is bad, then you miss out on the many potential benefits and gifts you can glean from your child's particular behavior.

In the first place, what is the meaning of the word 'will'? Merriam Webster defines 'will' as "an expression of strong desire, choice, willingness, consent or in negative constructions, refusal." I like this definition of the word far better than other definitions, such as that of the American Psychological Association, which states that will is "the capacity to make choices and determine their own behaviors in spite of influences external to them." In the latter definition, there is much more emphasis on cognition and the conscious decision to determine choices. While this may refer to the will, it isn't as adequate as the Webster definition. Yes, cognition plays a vital role in our decision-making process. But 'strong desire' can also contribute to other choices. In fact, some of the behavior of strong-willed children are borne more out of strong desires rather than well-thought-of decisions.

As we can see in some of the characteristics of strong-willed children, they are really driven by a goal. They are forward-thinking, always anticipating what is going to happen to them. In our anecdote at the beginning of the chapter, Emma is so intent on drawing. She has some vision of what her drawing would be and she is determined to capture that with her crayons. In that sense, strong-willed children are goal-oriented. Compare this with other children who lack goals or are very indecisive. And, because they do not have a goal they want to achieve, they find it tough to commit to anything.

With that goal in mind, strong-willed children will try to pursue their desires to the end. Emma will forgo cleaning her room just to finish her masterpiece. We might worry much about the general cleanliness of the house or we can focus on Emma's inflexibility. But we also have to commend her dedication to her work. We have to appreciate the strong-willed child's commitment to the goal in spite of many challenges that may derail them. Compare this to other children who easily give up on their goals. These children are not motivated to go beyond their hardships and work hard for something they really want. In this sense, we have to praise the child's willfulness to succeed.

Another commendable attitude of strong-willed children is self-determination. They are not reliant on others to accomplish something. If they want to learn a new sport or practice a new skill, they are going to find ways to fulfill it. This might even be at the cost of putting on a tantrum just to get what they want. They don't wait for an adult to take them to school or to do their homework for them. You have to appreciate the confidence they have in their ability to accomplish their objectives. Other children will simply wait passively until they are fed or taught anything. The active pursuit of a goal brings out the strengths of a strong-willed child.

Too Strong a Will

But anything in excess can be destructive, as in the case of strong-willfulness. While it may be commendable for some children to have an uncanny sense of independence, determination to pursue a goal and grit to withstand all challenges, being strong-willed may also negatively affect children. The fact that you are constantly wrestling or arguing with them does not justify this trait's positive outcomes. Certain developmental problems may persist with this trait which can impede the child from being disciplined and fully integrating with other children.

A large part of the problem may come from developmental dissonance. This refers to the idea that a certain trait may not be developmentally appropriate for a child. The positive characteristics of being willful would, in fact, suit an adult more. We say that a person with strong willpower can overcome all challenges to pursue their goals. An adult with a strong will believes in his talents and learns independently. Being willful is a trait we expect from mature adults.

But in children, being strong-willed may not be the most desired of traits. Not many parents would desire their children to be independent at such a young age. This is because the child is still in the process of maturation. The child's brain is far less advanced than the adult's. Being willful comes from many years of learning from past experiences. There is more deliberateness in the making of decisions because the adult has gone through a lifelong process of weighing options, determining possibilities, and understanding consequences. The child can only make decisions based on the limited experiences and learning opportunities they have. They may not make the best possible decision since they lack the many cognitive capacities that adults possess.

The goal is to develop willful adults who are capable of determining themselves and trusting in their abilities. But this only evolves as a process, a part of a continuum. At the far end of that continuum are children just starting to learn something about life. They are slowly developing their mental faculties to make optimal decisions. As parents, we do want our children to be independent someday. But it should not happen overnight. We cannot expect our kids to be determined about their future as early as six years old. We have to help them ease through this process one step at a time.

In fact, being too strong-willed as a child can impede a child's mental growth. If they are already fixed on one goal through one method, then their brains may be limited to discover other goals or the same goal through different methods. If the child decides to become a ballerina no matter what, then they may deprive themselves of developing other skills and other interests beyond their chosen goal. We cannot totally applaud the child's growing ability to manipulate devices when they function poorly in other areas. A child may insist on watching television, but we know better how this addicting behavior can stagnate their maturing brain. As much as we appreciate the positive attributes of being strong-willed, we cannot completely wish it to be fully developed in children.

What Makes My Child Strong-Willed?

How does a child become strong-willed? Why are some children more strong-willed than others? I get a lot of these questions from parents who are trying to understand their child's condition. It can be quite confusing for parents to attribute their child's traits. One parent tells me, "My husband and I were neither like that when we were kids. We don't know where she got it from." Another would tell me, "She must have gotten it from her father's side. His parents are as stubborn as their granddaughter." It becomes then a blaming game of whose side the undesirable trait came from.

Willfulness is an aspect of one's personality. The term 'personality' then encapsulates all these different traits a person may have into a wider, more cohesive framework. According to the American Psychological Association, personality refers to the dynamic and enduring patterns of feeling, thinking, and behaving an individual may uniquely have. Each one has a different personality that makes the individual incomparable to other people.

Two things stand out from this definition: personality is dynamic and enduring. Being dynamic, our personalities may be influenced by certain experiences we have in our lifetime. A death in the family may impact a child differently from an adult. Our daily experiences can shape the way we think, feel, and behave. But on the other hand, personality is also enduring. While we encounter many experiences, there are certain patterns of thinking, feeling, and behaving that endure throughout our lifetime. This may have stemmed from our childhood that we carry over to our lives as adults. This may include being willful. Strong-willed adults may have also been strong-willed children.

Over the years, many theorists have proposed different hypotheses on what makes us what we are.

Sigmund Freud postulated that personalities may have evolved over psychosexual stages (Lantze, 2021), while Alex Bandura advocated a social learning approach to personality. These different theories try to cover the complexity of what makes us who we are. But in general, different factors contribute to the makeup of the personality of our children. These include temperament, parenting styles, significant stress, and social interactions.

Temperament

Mary Rothbart (2006) defined temperament as individual differences in our regulation of emotion, activity, and attention during infancy and childhood. We react to stress differently and this can already be seen in infancy. This points to the idea that our temperaments may be biologically determined. A child may predominantly be fearful or frustrated, happy or distracted. Being strong-willed may have a biological basis.

This might mean that personality is something we also inherit from our parents. The claim that "it must be from your mother/father's side" has a certain truth to it, since we inherit some of our parent's temperaments through our genes. The strong-willed gene may not yet be identified, but we can say that we might have gotten that trait from our parents. Positive or negative traits can be passed through generations.

But this does not mean that we are determined to be exactly like our parents. Just because they are strong-willed does not always mean their children will be. Temperament is a good theory, but it is not a causal fact that can doom us for life. What we need to emphasize here is that our personality may be influenced by our parents which we can pass on to our children.

Parenting Styles

The way we raise our children also has an effect on their personalities. Bi et al. (2018) postulated that most parents adopt a particular pattern of raising their children which impacts their growth and personality. According to these experts, there are four patterns of parenting which we need to be aware of. It might be good for us to look at our own parenting styles and which of the four we can identify most with.

Authoritarian

These types of parents have very strong, dominant ways of raising their children. They create rules which they expect the children to conform to without questions. Authoritarian parents wield their power as adults and make children passive receivers of their commands. There is less room for compromise as these parents expect utmost obedience from their children. They use punishments more often to get their children to obey them. In turn, children who have authoritarian parents tend to have lower self-esteem since they may feel that their opinions are not valued. These children may become aggressive as the anger they nurse for their parents are repressed through their growing years. They avoid punishment, so they may tend to lie and put a good face on for their parents. The combination of active and passive aggression may lead children to disobey rules secretly.

Authoritative

These parents also enforce rules and discipline in the house. But they also consider the opinions and feelings of the child. They try to explain the reason behind each rule. They can be firm and mete out punishment when limits are crossed. But they will also explain why such punishments were given. Children of authoritative parents tend to be happier and more successful later on in life. They feel that their opinions and feelings are valid and attended to. There is room for compromise and they may feel empowered to make their own decisions.

Permissive

Parents with a permissive parenting style often set rules but rarely enforce them. They are more lenient towards their children. The approach is more of a friend rather than a parent, where the adults let children decide if they wish to follow their rules. They refrain from intervening too much with their child's affairs. They'll step back and let their child take a more active role. Children of permissive parents may be strong-willed. Too much leniency can be prone to abuse, and some children may grow up to be spoiled, expecting to have their way all the time.

Uninvolved

These parents neither make rules nor are they interested in their children's feelings and thoughts. They somehow expect the child to manage themselves with minimal or even total absence of adult supervision. There is less attention given to children as the adults are more preoccupied with their own concerns. Even if the issue is severe, the parents will not step in as they expect their child to resolve the issue on their own. Children of uninvolved parents tend to do poorly in school. Because their needs are not attended to, these children feel neglected and have poor self-esteem. With no adults to correct them, behavioral problems may arise.

These are just broad pictures of some patterns of parenting styles. We have to note here that the kind of parenting children receive will significantly affect how they are going to think, feel and behave. Hence, being strong-willed may be a reaction to authoritarian, permissive, or uninvolved parenting styles. If we are not conscious of our own tendencies to raise our children, we may not notice the great impact we are making on their personalities. As parents, we must recognize that what we do and say and how we make our children feel will shape their character, including being strong-willed.

Significant Stress

One of the most powerful determinants of personality is stress. We all experience various forms and degrees of stress in our lifetime. Our bodies are equipped with mechanisms to protect us from the harmful effects of these stressors. These are what we call coping mechanisms which prevent our physical and psychological state from deteriorating. This puts us in a 'fight or flight' response. We either confront the stressor head on, or we seek ways to avoid it altogether. When you feel hungry, your protective mechanism is to seek food. For children, hunger is a stressor that pushes them to cry, alerting the parent to feed them. When an adult sees a bus coming right at them, the protective mechanism kicks in to place themselves out of harm's way. When a baby sees a stranger, they cry so that they can alert the parent to protect them from an unknown danger. These protective mechanisms stay and evolve with us as we encounter different stressors.

The mental resources of children, however, are still evolving. Their capacity to protect themselves from overwhelming stressors is limited to a certain degree. Thus they are more vulnerable when negative events happen to them. This impacts the way they think, feel and behave about themselves and their environment. Children exposed to frequent or severe forms of stress may develop coping mechanisms which protect them from the immediate impact of the stressor. But these coping mechanisms may stay with the child even beyond the immediate danger and can form maladapted behaviors even in adulthood. For example, children who come from orphanages with poor resources may develop hoarding behaviors which allow them to survive during their time in the institution. But as adults who can work and support themselves, the hoarding behavior persists.

In a way, being strong-willed can be construed as a form of coping mechanism for some children. They may have experienced various forms of stressors that made them more goal-oriented, self-reliant, and stubborn than most children. Past experiences may have influenced their thinking, feeling, and behavioral patterns that make them bossy or more aggressive than other children.

One form of significant stress on children is experiencing divorce in the family. When children see their parents fighting, they are overwhelmed with many feelings that they cannot process. When one parent leaves them, children feel abandoned and rejected. They may even feel guilty for causing the breakup. This makes children turn the anger at their parents and their guilt into coping mechanisms that strengthen their self-reliance. If adults can't be trusted, children will have to rely on themselves. They will be adamant about practicing a certain activity in order to strengthen themselves.

Another significant life stressor is addiction and violence in the family. This can be in the form of alcoholism or drug abuse. Under the influence of these dangerous substances, the father can inflict physical harm on the wife and/or the children. This creates a deep trauma in children when they see their inebriated father hitting their mother or their siblings. As a form of coping with the violence, children might transform their anger against their father into self-determination. Even as children, they may feel the need to protect their mother and so they can be stubborn or aggressive towards others.

These and other negative events, such as deaths in the family, poverty, unemployment, war, or conflict among others, can make a lasting impact on children. What we perceive as misbehavior can in fact be a form of coping mechanism they developed as means of protecting themselves from these trauma. It is very important for us to protect children from these negative effects. But since we cannot totally prevent these from happening, we have to process the thoughts and feelings of children because this may translate to behaviors that are hard to correct later on. Remember that in any stressful event, it is always the child who is most affected.

There are other determinants of personality that can explain the presence of the strong-willed trait in children. We will tackle more of them in the next chapters. But it is sufficient for us to understand that both 'nature and nurture' elements are present. Being strong-willed may have been inherited, but a large part of that trait comes from the life experiences of children that shape the way they think, feel, and behave.

Chapter 2

Neurodevelopmental Issues

Ms. Davis was quite fond of her first-grade class. She had a total of fifteen kids, all cute and eager to learn. Teaching was her passion, and she loved it when kids learned something new each day. She spent a lot of time designing her lessons to make them more interesting for children. This weekend, she effortfully cut out several animal pictures from different magazines. She knew that kids especially liked it when she had colorful visuals.

"Good morning class!" She greeted them on a cheery Monday morning.

"Good morning Ms. Davis," they all chimed in.

"Today, I am going to show you some pictures of animals you see in the wild. Can you tell me what the names of these cute animals are?" She took out a picture of an angry-looking creature.

Manuel raised his hands, "Teacher, that's a polar bear."

"Very good, Manuel. Yes, it's a polar bear and they live in very cold temperatures. Ok, next. What do you call this animal?" She raised the picture of an animal covered up in feathers.

Again Manuel's hands were quickly raised. "Thank you, Manuel, but maybe we can give others a chance. How about you Carly, do you know what this animal is?"

"That's an American eagle!" Manuel said aloud even before Carly could say anything.

"Thank you, Manuel. But I think we should respect our classmates when it's their turn to speak up. We should give others a chance to talk, don't you think?" She said testily.

"Yes, Ms. Davis." Manuel said obediently.

As the class went on, Manuel kept on interrupting the class by saying the right answer to Ms. Davis' questions out loud. The other kids remained silent as Manuel dominated the discussion. Ms. Davis knew Manuel was quite difficult to work with and decided just to move to the next part of the lesson.

"Ok. Now that we got to know some animals, I want you now to take out your crayons and drawing materials. I will give you some time to draw your favorite animal. It could be a cat, a dog, or your pet turtle. Color your favorite animal and sign your drawing. At the end of our class, everyone will share your drawing and explain what you have drawn and why it is your favorite animal. Is that clear?" Ms. Davis said.

"Yes, teacher!" The kids said eagerly. They proceeded to draw their favorite animals quietly. Carly was drawing his cat with blue crayons. Alfred was sketching a monkey. Ms. Davis walked around the class, peeking through each child's progress.

Just after five minutes, Manuel said aloud "I'm finished!" And he raised his paper.

Ms. Davis said, "That's good, Manuel. Kindly take your seat and just wait quietly while your other classmates finish." She moved on to examining the work of other children.

No sooner did she turn her attention to Alfred, when Ms. Davis heard a ruckus at the back. There was

Manuel running to and from at the back, knocking over the other children's bags.

"Manuel, please go back to your chair." Ms. Davis commanded. "If you are finished with your work, let the other children finish their work. One more misbehavior and I will have to send you on time-out," she threatened.

But Manuel just couldn't help but feel restless. He started to tap his feet on the ground noisily, creating a repetitive noise. He couldn't keep still and now, he was banging on his chair as he began singing "Old MacDonald had a farm…"

Ms. Davis was quite lost. There were fourteen other children who wanted to learn. But it seemed she had been spending too much time controlling Manuel, who seemed oblivious to his classmates. Ms. Davis thought she had to call Manuel's parents.

It was beyond Ms. Davis' competence to handle Manuel's misbehavior. Maybe, she could understand his situation better if she had listened to his parents. But for the time being, she could only plead for Manuel to calm down and give the rest of the class a break.

Do you worry that your child may be more strong-willed than other children? There might not be such a thing as a perfectly compliant child who will obey your every command 100% of the time. Your child may carry out most of your requests, but they may have moody days when they tend to resist. But do you have a feeling that your child may be more aggressive and stubborn than usual? It might be good to have them screened for certain neurodevelopmental disorders.

Why Check for Neurodevelopmental Disorders?

When you have a suspicion that your child may be more different than other children in terms of extremes in behavior, it would be to the child's advantage if they get screened earlier. In 2016, the United States Centers for Disease Control and Prevention said that 6.1 million or 9.4% of American children had been diagnosed with attention deficit hyperactivity disorder or ADHD. In 2016, the CDC reported that "one in every 54 children" is diagnosed with an autism spectrum disorder or ASD.

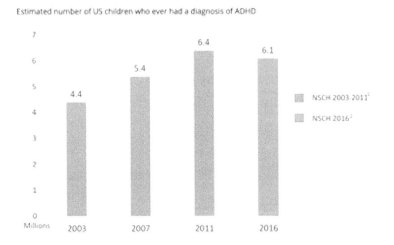

Estimated number of US children who ever had a diagnosis of ADHD

https://www.cdc.gov/ncbddd/adhd/data.html

These data only refer to diagnosed cases of ASD and ADHD. We do not have knowledge of the true prevalence of these conditions. We can only imagine how many more kids are undiagnosed and are suffering from these conditions. Neurodevelopmental disorders are rising as more parents are more open to consulting with professionals regarding their child's condition.

Parents are quite reluctant to screen their children for ASD and ADHD because of the negative connotations these conditions hold. I've heard some parents say, "My child is not autistic. He's just too energetic." There are even others who say, "ADHD is just a convenient term for lazy parents to blame a medical condition for poor parenting." I resent these claims because they reflect a poor understanding of ASD and ADHD. It might be painful to accept that your child may have these conditions. It is your child who will benefit if they get to be diagnosed and treated earlier. What is good with screening for these conditions is that timely interventions can be enacted if the conditions are diagnosed earlier. There are a lot of professionals who can help you understand and care for your child better. These conditions greatly rely on parental care and supervision. But if you know the medical diagnosis, you can have access to other professional resources of support to help the child cope with himself and his environment. Let us now try to understand ASD and ADHD and check if your child might have some symptoms that warrant further investigation. Again, this will benefit your child more if you have more information.

Autism Spectrum Disease

Autism spectrum disorder is characterized by two major dysfunctions in development: challenges in social communication and engaging in repetitive or restrictive patterns of behavior (APA, 2013). What you notice as stubbornness or being strong-willed may be symptoms of a failure of the child to communicate exactly what they need. Children with ASD often have trouble with language and communication. There is

a tendency to use gestures and hand signs instead
of words to indicate their requests. And they can get
very frustrated when people don't understand what
they want. There is this one parent who shared with
me how her son would take her hand and nudge it
in a certain direction. She didn't understand what it
meant and the poor kid was so frustrated that his mom
could not get his message. Later on, she realized that
he was using her hand to point to a cookie jar and
that he wanted a chocolate chip cookie. It can be very
frustrating for both parents and children with ASD to
convey their commands and requests. Eye contact is
also poor. There is less interest in interacting with
other children because they are preoccupied with
their own interests. At times, they display emotions
that are incongruent to the situation. For example,
when they go to a funeral, they might burst into
laughter or say something awkward. This is because
they have low receptivity for social cues. They cannot
recognize other people's emotions and how this might
be appropriate or not in a certain situation.

Another aspect of ASD is engaging in repetitive
behavior. You will see children with ASD lining up
bottles, pencils, crayons, or any random material.
They may have repetitive gestures like scratching
their eyes, rolling their hands, or tapping their feet.
Certain rituals are strictly observed, like always
washing hands or eating certain colors of food only.

When these rituals are not followed, they get angry easily. They feel lost and afraid when the patterns that comfort them are not followed. What we see as inflexibility in children may be signs of restrictive patterns that children with ASD exhibit.

Studies have not been conclusive with regards to the causes of ASD. Advanced maternal age or genetic predisposition are some areas of interest that show association with the incidence of ASD (Werling, 2018). But these theories have yet to be proven with high causality. It is unfair for parents to blame themselves just because their child has ASD. As some parents would say to me, "We are just more lucky to have a child with ASD." You never know if you will have a child with ASD, so it might be useless to dwell on blaming yourself for their condition.

Attention Deficit Hyperactivity Disorder

Like ASD, children diagnosed with attention deficit and hyperactivity disorder have difficulty with two major areas of functionality. The very name of the condition already indicates these domains: attention and hyperactivity (Silber, 2004). They may look like seemingly normal children full of energy but too much of it might be an indication of a developmental condition.

First, children with ADHD have low attention spans. They lose their things easily or they overlook details frequently. Of course, nobody is perfect and children often make mistakes. It might be harder to spot a child with ADHD from someone who has learning disabilities, in language or mathematics for example. What sets them apart is that children with ADHD actually have high aptitude and capacity to learn. They have poor grades because they cannot concentrate on the material in front of them. They have trouble following directions, especially multi-step ones, since they are unable to focus. There is a tendency for these children to be often sidetracked by random objects that distract them from their school work. More frequently, teachers catch children with ADHD earlier than parents because inattention is more obviously seen in school performance.

Next, the level of energy and activity of children with ADHD is far higher than normal children. They have difficulty waiting in line or sitting on a chair. They feel a certain restlessness when they are stuck in a particular place. In the anecdote at the beginning of this chapter, we see Manuel frequently interrupting his teacher and speaking out of turn. He also cannot sit for prolonged periods because it makes him anxious. It is really difficult to screen children with ADHD on the basis of hyperactivity because children are naturally inquisitive and have high energy. Nevertheless, we may have a higher index of suspicion for children who display outbursts of restlessness and talkativeness more often than most kids.

Like ASD, we do not know exactly what causes ADHD. Again, the combination of genetics and the environment may affect the development of ADHD (Dobie, 2012). But we also have to debunk certain myths about getting ADHD. It is not true that feeding children too much sugar causes hyperactivity (CDC, 2006). It may only contribute to the already existing condition. Until there are sufficient data to pinpoint the cause, we do not need to punish ourselves for inducing ADHD in children. Instead, we can use more of that energy into looking for help for our children.

The Role of Professionals

While I have just described some common features of ASD and ADHD, this should not assume any diagnosis yet. What I have detailed are just some common symptoms of these conditions which could alert parents to a possible neurodevelopmental condition. It is still best to see a professional in order to make an accurate diagnosis. These professionals have dedicated their lives to studying, and they've received the education and training necessary to recognize specific problems associated with these conditions that other parents may miss. They are licensed to administer and interpret tests like the Modified Checklist for Autism in Toddlers (M-CHAT), Autism Diagnostic Interview-Revised (ADI-R) (Corsello, 2007), or the Vanderbilt ADHD diagnostic rating scale (Smith, 2007), which may diagnose your child with more accuracy.

The prognosis for children with neurodevelopmental disorders is not reassuring. Much of the problem lies in the delayed diagnosis of the condition. Sometimes, parents are so reluctant to seek professional help that the critical stages for language and social skills acquisition have already passed. Parents may be ashamed of having a child with autism or are just optimistic that they will outgrow their behavior even if they don't seek timely help. Consequently, this leads to a more severe form of ASD and ADHD, which could impair the child for life.

Management of these conditions includes a combination of pharmacologic and non-pharmacologic interventions. Some children with intense hyperactivity may be given anxiety-reducing drugs which can counter the hormonal imbalance they are experiencing. The focus is on making the child more functional. Therapies target the enhancement of the child's capacity to learn in school and to communicate with their caregivers and peers. Children are taught to handle their emotions and to be reflective of their actions.

We also have to be realistic in our expectations of the prognosis of our children. Not one drug or therapy will completely eradicate the condition. In fact, medical and functional therapies may have to be sustained for life. It can be depressing and frustrating for parents who expect their children with ASD and ADHD to function normally like other children. It will take some effort and patience from us, parents. Ultimately, it is the home environment that will determine the survival and growth of these children. When parents provide adequate support and love to their children, the effects of these conditions can be mitigated.

Whether your child has been diagnosed with ADHD or ASD or not, the following chapters may be helpful to parents in understanding and caring for their strong-willed children. Now that we know what our children may be going through, we can move on to learning how to assist them in life the best way possible.

Chapter 3

The Most Effective Approach

"Dan, I think it's time for you to do your homework." Roger chided his son in between switching channels. The New England Patriots were playing tonight, and it was bound to be a close game against the Pittsburgh Steelers.

"Um, Dad, can I just do it tomorrow morning? It's pretty easy and I can finish it real quick." Dan bargained.

"What's with the delay, bud? It's easier if you do your homework tonight, so you don't have to worry about anything tomorrow. I don't like you rushing crazily in the morning." The game was starting and Roger was trying to focus on the opening.

"But I'm not in the mood to do my homework right now." Dan could be quite stubborn. He wasn't exactly the best in class, but he managed to pass. A little homework undone wouldn't hurt once in a while, he figured.

"Just do your homework, just like any other normal kid." Roger raised the volume of the television a little bit. "Don't make it difficult for me. I'm sure your other classmates are doing their homework right now. You don't want to miss out on the fun they're having, do you?" Roger teased.

"But Dad! Marvin and Keith aren't doing their homework either. Their dads let them watch the television with them, even during school nights. If they are allowed to skip homework, why can't I?" Dan was trying to shout over the television volume.

"Well, I'm not Marvin or Keith's dad. You're in my house, so you play by my rules. And I say you should do your homework now. If they can get away with it, I won't permit it here. It's for your own good, and I think Marvin and Keith should learn that too." Roger was still glued to the TV screen but he could sense anger brewing in Dan's corner.

"You're always watching television. Why can't I also watch television and not do my homework? It's not fair!" Dan said determinedly. He started to pout and crossed his hands.

"Until you become an adult, then you have to follow me. School's good for you, and you can watch all the television you want after you finish school. I'm finding it hard to concentrate on this game with you whining around. Just go to your room and finish your homework." Roger said.

"No. It's not fair. I don't want to do my homework and you can't make me." Dan stomped off in a corner, trying to watch the game as well.

"You really want me to do this huh? If that's what you want, then sure thing." Roger turned off the television. Father and son stared blankly at the screen while the awkward silence filled the room.

"I can do this all night, bud. I'm telling you, just finish your homework and you can sit here beside me if you're finished. The earlier you do it, the sooner you can watch the games. You wouldn't want to miss out on halftime, would you?" Roger bribed his son.

"No. If I can't watch it, then so can't you. That's fair." Dan stubbornly proclaimed.

Roger could only look at his son fuming back at him. He wanted desperately to watch the game, but Dan was making it doubly hard for the both of them. They both stared at each other, neither party wanting to give up their egos.

How do we actually help our children who are strong-willed? It might be difficult for us to do anything about our child's temperament, given the strong genetic nature of this factor. We also cannot totally prevent stressful events from happening. The greatest impact we can make a difference in is in the quality and manner of our parenting. The role of the family plays a central figure in the development of childhood traits like being strong-willed. We have to understand how great an impact we have on our children's thoughts, feelings, and behaviors.

The Impact of Our Parenting

We have seen in the first chapter how different parenting styles like being authoritarian, authoritative, permissive, or uninvolved can impact children's personalities. How parents relate with their children influences the child's thoughts, emotions, and behaviors. Because parents and siblings are the child's first and dominant contacts to the world, the child's experiences with the family will translate how they will view the world as children and as adults. We need to dwell on how exactly this happens.

Our behaviors are influenced by our thoughts and emotions. We cannot read thoughts or assume emotions simply by looking at a person. Behavior then is the outward manifestation of a person's internal thoughts and feelings. When you hear your child saying, "I don't want to go to school," that external behavior is reflective of an internal thought and/or an emotion. Maybe the child is stubborn because they feel afraid of someone in class or they think that they will fail in a subject. So our thoughts and feelings are manifested only in behavior. Thus, we will focus our discussion on how parents impact the child's thoughts and feelings.

Modeling

How do we actually learn? How did we learn our first words? How did we learn to eat with a spoon and fork? It might be helpful for us to explore certain theories that could exactly explain how we learn. One of the foremost learning theorists is Albert Bandura, who proposed the Social Learning Theory. According to Bandura (1963), learning happens as a cognitive process of observing and imitating others. The social context is very important in this theory, suggesting that we do not learn anything from a vacuum but only through a particular context. For example, if somebody tells you to build a "saputi," what would you do? Without a social context, you wouldn't know what a "saputi" is or if it's a verb, a noun, or an adjective. We don't know what it is just by the very word because we don't have a context for it. But if an Inuit from Alaska demonstrates to you that a "saputi" is a kind of fishing technique they use by utilizing a stone dam to trap fish (Travel Nunavut, 2021), you can have an idea of what "saputi" is. We can only learn something if there is some sort of social context on which to base our observations.

Bandura called the entire process of social learning as modeling. He emphasized that modeling is composed of four important and different cognitive processes which we use to learn anything. This will be helpful for us to understand exactly how children learn.

Attention

In order for a child to learn, he must first pay attention to the parent doing the action. If the kid is not focused or distracted, the behavior that is being demonstrated will go unnoticed and unabsorbed. When you want to teach your child how to speak, it might be good to open your mouth as wide as possible so that the child could notice how the mouth opens out to produce a sound. When you are teaching your kid to wave goodbye, the child notices your hands flapping quickly in a side-to-side motion.

Retention

From the sensory information about the behavior to be learned, the brain then stores this into memory. We have different storages in the brain for memory, including short- or long-term. For example, the child can remember the shape of the mouth as his father is speaking "apple." He can even remember what the word sounds like. This memory will help him say "apple" on his own. In another case, a child may recall associating a side-to-side motion of the hands with the sound of "goodbye."

Reproduction

After that, the child does these activities himself. He accesses his brain's recollection of the behavior and translates it to his body. The memory of his mother mouthing "Mama" is imitated by the child. The child recalls the motion of goodbye and proceeds to wave his own hands from side to side. We can only know if the behavior is learned if the child can repeat it without prompt.

Motivation

The child has now learned the behavior, either saying "Mama" or waving goodbye. Now, the imitation of these behaviors is dependent on whether the child is motivated to use these actions in a particular context. The child will say "Mama" only when he sees and hears his mother. He won't say "Mama" when a stranger arrives. The child uses the goodbye gesture when somebody is leaving. He won't use that gesture when he is hungry or he feels sleepy. The context then is important for behaviors to be enacted.

These four processes – attention, retention, reproduction and motivation – ensure that a certain behavior is cognitively encoded and learned before it is translated to objective action. The child learns by observing the parent, committing the behavior to memory, trying it out for himself and producing it in an appropriate context. Thereby, a child cannot learn any behavior that the parent does not exhibit.

Bandura's modeling theory highlights the role of parents in stimulating children's cognitive development and learning. Children will always imitate their parents. If they hear their father curse, then they will repeat the word. If their mother hugs them often, children will also be expressive huggers. In the anecdote we have at the start of the chapter, we see Dan being very stubborn about doing his homework. But when we look at Roger's behavior, we can understand that Dan is simply imitating his dad's actions. We cannot totally blame Dan for being stubborn because he is simply mirroring his father's behavior of being focused on the television game. We have to be careful with which actions we display to our children because this is going to be imitated. Parents are the role models for their children.

Processing of Emotions

We can also apply Bandura's social learning of behavior to modeling of emotions. Castro et al. (2015) proposed a theory that explains how parents process emotions which children imitate. Like Bandura, these researchers recognized how children take after their parents. But these proponents underscored that the reactions of parents to certain situations influence how children deal with different emotions. When children feel sad, happy, afraid, or angry, they will look up to their parents on how to handle and display these emotions.

The ability of children to recognize and deal with their emotions greatly influences the coping mechanisms they will develop to different stressors, including being strong-willed. Castro et al. outlined three different factors which can affect a child's emotional recognition skills.

Parents' Beliefs

The belief of parents towards different emotions is transmitted to their children. If parents believe that emotions are valuable, they will make their children aware of how both positive and negative feelings are normal and valid. When you demonstrate your happiness when receiving a gift to your children, your children will learn that expressing happiness is normal. If you demonstrate crying when you lose someone you love, your children will understand that it is okay to cry.

But if parents think that emotions are dangerous or problematic, they might hide or mask their own emotions to protect children from negative emotions. You want to shield your children from your sadness, so you always put on a happy face. Without these social cues, there is no opportunity for children to learn about emotions, and they may be left to guess what their parents are feeling. Children will not be guided as to how important and normal feelings are when their parents do not express and explain the context of these emotions.

Parent's Socialization

For Castro et al. (2015), parents have a great impact on how their children process these feelings. Parents are actually tasked to guide their children on how to make sense of these emotions. One specific skill is labeling. Parents must be able to identify the particular emotion being felt in a given situation. When a child loses a pet, parents may tell the child that the emotion they are feeling is 'sadness' or 'longing.' When parents don't even attempt to name feelings, then children may experience these emotions without having a handle on what they are exactly feeling.

Teaching is another essential skill that parents should possess. This refers to guiding children on the causes and consequences of a certain emotional event. Parents should take the time to explain that the child is feeling sad because his pet is important to him and that the pet is now gone. The child can appreciate how loving someone or something can bring about both positive and negative feelings. Parents should also teach the consequences of actions. If the child pushes a neighbor, the parents should guide the child on how his action impacts the other person's emotion. Because you pushed him, he felt hurt and angry. When children's feelings are processed, they can understand how their behaviors also affect other people. When children are not taught about processing their emotions, they might not recognize how their aggression or strong-willfulness can impact other people.

We can never overemphasize that children's cognitive and emotional learning is highly dependent upon their parents. As much as you want to change your child's misbehavior, you also have to recognize how your own actions may have influenced his thinking and feeling. We need to be aware that our children are looking up to us as their role models. The strong willfulness they are exhibiting may reflect some of our own deficiencies to understand and process our thoughts and emotions. We can visualize this in the following diagram:

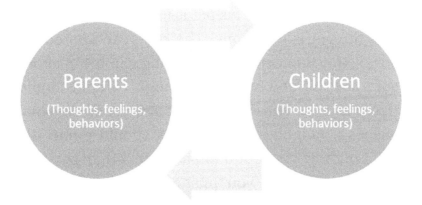

We see here how our thoughts, feelings, and behaviors influence our children's thoughts, feelings, and behaviors. But the process is not one-sided. Our children are also capable of influencing us. When they are throwing a tantrum, we must recognize that their actions trigger us, and we feel angry. When our children are excited and happy about a camping trip that we are planning, we also feel happy and giddy at such an event. Your children are triggering your emotions and thoughts all the time. Certainly, we have to recognize that we have the primary agency of molding our children's thoughts, feelings, and behaviors as adults. But as humans, we are also capable of being influenced by our children.

An Empathic Framework for Raising Strong-Willed Children

Let me propose to you a simple framework for raising strong-willed children. Taking everything we have learned so far, we direct our parenting then towards an orientation of empathy. Our goal is not to make children weak-willed or lacking in will. The opposite of stubbornness and being strong-willed is not necessarily being pushovers and weaklings. Our aim is not to develop children who will simply obey our every command without thinking for themselves. Rather, we want to make our children more empathetic and loving.

What does empathy even mean? The Greek word 'pathos' means 'to suffer' while the preposition 'em' means 'with'. Taken together, empathy then means 'to suffer with' (Harper, n.d.). It means that we are able to put ourselves in the shoes of another person so that we can imagine their worldview. We feel empathy for the homeless we see in the street when we can imagine how they must be feeling. Empathy is an important virtue to teach our children and the cornerstone of our society. It is in fact, the antidote to strong-willfulness.

Rogers et al. (2007) expanded the notion of empathy beautifully. They say that empathy is actually composed of three aspects: cognitive, affective, and somatic. We will discuss each aspect and apply this to parenthood.

Cognitive Empathy

When we can expand our thinking and reimagine what others are thinking, we are practicing cognitive empathy. If I tell you, "Imagine a peaceful beach with seagulls chirping and the sun setting slowly," what image would you have in mind? At that very instant, we are sharing a similar but not exactly the same image. The beach in my mind might be in Australia while yours is a festive Rio de Janeiro beach.

This is very important to teach our children who may be strong-willed. Usually, these children have a very definite way of doing things according to their perspective. But if we can expand that perspective and invite our children to view the world in a different way, then we are expanding their perspective. They become less strong-willed when they can understand how other people think about the situation.

In the same way, we should also practice cognitive empathy ourselves. Rather than just tell your children what they should be doing, it might also be a good idea to understand where they are coming from. If you are concerned about their behavior, you might want to imagine the thought process behind that and reach some understanding of their condition. You might have a broader understanding if you listen to the perspective of others. The very process of understanding changes you.

Affective Empathy

When we are able to feel what others are going through, then we are using affective empathy. If you see someone crying at a funeral, your heart goes out to them and you feel their sadness too. It may not be as intense as the other person, but you have a sense of the emotion that they are feeling. You might not have an experience of a loved one dying, but you could probably relate to an experience of losing something you love. In this way, you are able to connect to the feelings of others by tapping into yours.

Teaching children how to imagine the feelings of other people is important in softening strong-willfulness. These children may be so consumed by their own emotions that they feel impatient, bossy, and demanding. But if you lead them to understand the feelings of others, then their stubbornness may give way to understanding. Maybe when your strong-willed child feels how shouting and kicking can be irritating and hurting other people, they may be led to stop those behaviors.

In the same way, we should also try to feel what our children are feeling. Whenever they are throwing a tantrum, perhaps it is good to imagine the frustration they must be feeling. This exercise allows you to move away from your own frustration. It may make you more sympathetic about your child's concerns. You might be less angry at your child when you are able to feel their inability to express their emotions appropriately.

Somatic/Behavioral Empathy

Rogers et al. (2007) described somatic empathy as a physical reaction based on imagining the thoughts and feelings of others. I found this to be rather vague. I would rather use the term 'behavioral empathy' to refer to how our actions are guided by considering the thoughts and feelings of other people. Empathy is not just about thinking and feeling. It must lead you to certain actions. If you stop only at imagining how a homeless person thinks and feels without doing anything, then what is the use of empathy? Without actions, these thoughts and feelings are of no value.

We can then move towards addressing the behavioral concerns of our children when they are better able to understand their thoughts and emotions. As parents, we guide their behavior based on considering their own concerns as well as the concerns of other people. The stubborn behavior we used to see can give way to behaviors that are more considerate of the feelings of others. In the same way, our parenting should also take into account the feelings and thoughts of our children. From being bossy authority figures, perhaps we can grow in engaging our children in making their own decisions with our guidance.

The empathic approach to strong-willed children requires a change in our thinking, feeling, and behavior. As much as we want to change our children, we should also change ourselves in the process. This can be quite difficult with parents who are defensive about their own beliefs and reactions. This framework will not work for parents who are convinced that they do not need to grow and learn more about themselves. The empathic framework can actually be difficult and painful because it will question your own beliefs about yourself. This approach will lead you to be empathic as well. So from empathic parents, empathic children can be developed.

In the succeeding chapters, we will be discussing the four pillars of the empathic framework in caring for strong-willed children. The modules are designed to develop skills in both the parent and the child. Each will tackle a different aspect of empathy you can apply in your daily life. The pillars of the empathic framework include:

- Be present – This chapter will discuss how to pay more attention and be present with your child.

- Praise and Discipline – It is important to set rules in the household. This chapter will make you understand how positive and negative reinforcements can be strategically utilized.

- Learn in Play – Children enjoy play and this is central to the formation of their social skills. This chapter will discuss how you can both grow and learn from this enjoyable activity.

- Manage Your Emotions – Our emotions play an important role in explaining our behavior. This chapter will help you understand your child's and your own emotions.

These pillars of empathy are all needed to empower your child and yourself. Dwell on each chapter slowly and relish the many lessons you can learn. Each chapter begins with some points for reflection. Take that time to put aside the book and really reflect about how these points relate to your life. We will proceed to have a deeper understanding of each pillar. The chapter concludes with some useful exercises for you and your children. Move slowly so you can really understand each chapter. It is essential to read each chapter gradually and thoroughly. Your relationship with your child will not change overnight. But as you read the next chapter, work towards making your relationships stronger and more life-giving. Remember that you will also be changed by this process. Let the building begin!

Chapter 4

Growing in Being Present

"Jeremy, could you please stop hiding your brother's toys? It's getting annoying when your brother comes up to me every time you play a prank on him. Be a good brother, can you?" Mollie said exasperatedly. She expected so much more from Jeremy, her eldest, but she found herself constantly disappointed. Mollie wanted her elder son to be more responsible in looking after his younger brother, but she found Jeremy sorely lacking.

"But Mom, I didn't hide Luke's toy truck. I swear! Not this time" confessed Jeremy. He liked having a younger sibling, after some time being the only child.

But Jeremy just couldn't help but play pranks on his brother.

"Mommy, I think Jeremy stole my truck," whined baby Luke. "He takes my things and makes me cry."

"I am telling you Jeremy, if I don't have that toy truck in one minute, I'm going to ground you for a week. I have had enough of your tricks and I refuse to play games with you anymore. Where is Luke's toy truck? I want it now!" Mollie was almost screaming.

The constant fights between her children weren't exactly doing wonders for her health. She constantly felt stressed at home whenever her boys would break into fights. This was on top of the many things she had to accomplish, being a single mom. It was good that she could work from home, processing company documents while tending to her kids. But on bad days, the constant bickering of the boys gets on her nerves.

"Mom, I swear I didn't take it this time. I know I have played pranks on Luke before, but not this time. I didn't take his truck." Jeremy was indignant with his stand.

"I don't believe you for one second. You are always playing tricks on your brother, I've had enough of you. Just give me the truck and this will be over. Please, just do it for me." Mollie didn't want to continue begging to her children to obey her. It was getting tiring especially as she had a lot of other things on her mind.

"You're always accusing me of doing something bad. Yeah, maybe I do play tricks sometimes. But not all the time. I don't know where Luke's truck is. Even if you search my room, you won't find it anywhere. I'm not lying Mom, believe me just for once." Jeremy defended himself.

"I thought I could count on you as a big brother. But I'm pretty disappointed with you Jeremy. Pretty disappointed." Mollie exclaimed. And with that, Jeremy walked out to his room and slammed the door behind him.

"No supper for you, then," shouted Mollie.

She didn't know how to discipline her child anymore. Before, she could sweet talk Jeremy into doing anything. But now, he just wouldn't obey any of Mollie's requests. It was getting harder and harder to have him do anything. Mollie resigned herself to look for Luke's truck. Her small boy was still bawling his eyes out and Mollie just felt all the stress draining her dry. She just couldn't understand her children anymore.

Mollie continued cleaning the house. As she was arranging the books in the family room, she found Luke's toy truck neatly tucked away in one corner. She remembered that she had placed the truck there as a bookend.

"Oops!" She thought to herself.

Mollie felt a little guilty about blaming Jeremy. But it might seem too awkward to apologize now.

"And maybe he deserves this too for the many other times he played pranks," Mollie convinced herself.

Points for Reflection

- When was the last time I attended my child's school activity?

- What is my son's favorite food?

- Name three of your child's friends.

- What subject does your daughter have difficulty in?

- Is your child right or left-handed? Or ambidextrous?

- What does your child want to be when she grows up?

- When was the last time you had a family dinner with no gadgets?

- What sport or hobby is your child interested in?

- What flavor of ice-cream does your child adore?

Why Being Present Matters?

If you are able to answer most of the previous questions, then congratulations! You are at least updated with different details about your child. This might seem strange because we assume that parents know everything about their children. But you would be surprised that many parents may not be able to answer some or most of these questions.

The first pillar of the empathic framework is being present. You might think that this is quite a strange skill to learn since just being there is too simple. But your mere presence affects your child tremendously. It's crucial for a child's attachment development to have both parents present during his or her childhood. This refers to the affectionate bond between a child and a caregiver (Bretherton, 1992). The fragile baby has to establish secure bonds of intimacy with a stable caregiver for the child to be assured that the world is a safe place to be in.

Mary Ainsworth (1969) described this attachment theory as an instinctive process binding children with their caregivers. She believed that if parents consistently show presence and care for their children, the youngster will grow up to be confident and self-assured. But if parents develop avoidant, ambivalent, or disorganized patterns of attachment, children will grow up to be very suspicious about their surroundings. For example, if a mother abandons her child for prolonged periods of time, the child will learn to distrust the mother. The child might be suspicious if the mother will be gone again and leave him crying. This carries over to adulthood wherein the individual distrusts intimate relationships and are always wary they may be abandoned at anytime.

Children who are strong-willed may also have attachment or attention issues. Their stubbornness or aggressive behavior may be an acting out, a plea to be given attention to. The child is not being testy just to spite you or because they are intrinsically evil. Perhaps, they are acting that way because it is the only method they know which will catch your attention. Children crave to be loved by their parents. When not much attention is given to them, they will seek destructive ways such as throwing a tantrum, being passive-aggressive, or bullying other children. Even if they are reprimanded, they will at least feel that you care for them enough to scold them.

How Parents Can Develop the Skill

Here are some ways in which you can develop the valuable skill of being present. We may need to have an honest evaluation of ourselves so we can be open and improve our sense of being present to our children.

Giving Time

Time is perhaps one of the most precious gifts you can give your children. Oddly enough, it is also one of the hardest to give. We are pulled by so many demands from our different functions. Yes, we have our obligations to our families. But we also have responsibilities at work, with our friends and relatives, and even to ourselves. And I can sympathize with you. Families have different setups with regards to balancing the concerns of the home and with earning a living. There are families where one parent is working fulltime in the office or in a business, while the other parent stays at home with the children. There are families where both parents are working and they take turns taking care of the children. There are single-parent families who entrust the care of their children to relatives and extended family as they have to work. There are families who are fortunate enough to be able to work from home. But there are also families where one parent has to go abroad to earn a living and only returns home once or twice a year. These different setups can really make an impact on the child. You have to consider just how much your living and working arrangements can affect your ability to finance your expenses while giving your children due attention.

Sometimes, you can be physically there, but your spirit is somewhere else. You may be so preoccupied with the concerns of the work that even during dinnertime with the family, your thoughts are still on the projects you need to finish in the office. During weekends, you can be at home. But you just want to rest most of the time just to recover from the stress of the week. You might want to listen to your child's stories. But you may still need to do a lot of other things like washing the car, taking out the garbage, or fixing the leaky faucet. And children can sense this. They know when your full attention is on them or not. The quality of our being present may be compromised when we don't prioritize giving time for our children.

I don't blame you for managing all of your different responsibilities with your best efforts. But you also need to prioritize quality time for your children. They will only be kids for a short while. You may miss out on milestones in their lives if you are always out doing 'more important' things. You might not know who your child's friends may be or how they may be performing in school with your own concern for deadlines and appointments. If you value your children, you have to give them time.

It's not as if you have to be paying them full attention 24/7. A good one hour of being fully there with your kids is going to make them feel very important. Eating for an hour without gadgets may help you become abreast with how your child is doing in school. Cheering them on during swim meets or football games makes them more confident and appreciated. It won't cost you much to spare your children a few moments of your full undivided attention.

Observing

Being present for your child does not mean you have to engage them in conversation all the time. You don't need to play games or create various exciting activities just to bond with your children. Sometimes, all we need to do is just to observe our children. When we are observing, we shift from a mode of dominating the conversation with our opinions or commanding our children to do certain tasks. We also need times when we can just look at our child and appreciate different aspects of them as they play, do their homework, or even just when they are asleep.

Take time to notice different aspects of your child at any one point. Kids grow at such a tremendous pace that you may miss out on those tiny changes if you don't take time to observe. Does your child write with the right or the left hand? Do they eat their veggies or are they not too fond of these? What new words are they learning now? These tiny details are taken for granted as children grow up. But it might be good to document these milestones when observing your children. It will be a laugh when you revisit these memories when they grow up. Your children will appreciate these small gestures of attention. It tells them "I am important" or "My mom notices me." They won't need to act out if they feel that their actions don't go unnoticed.

Don't be selective when you are observing your child. Sometimes, we can only focus on the little that is wrong with them instead of the good they do more often. The only times we focus our attention on them is if they broke a vase, punched their little brother, or got lost in a shopping mall. The only times we may have visited them at school was when to get them out of detention. But if you really take time out to be with your child, you will notice that they are more disciplined, more amiable, and even more caring than you give them credit for. The few dramatic outbursts are more memorable to us than their everyday ordinary good behavior. And it is quite unfair to them. If you always focus on finding what's wrong with your child, then you will always see something to be mad at. But if you view your child as lovable in their unique ways, then you will notice all the good and not so good things they do in a larger perspective.

Listening

Again, the simplicity of the skill of listening can be misleading. It is hard to listen, especially to give your full attention to the endless banter of your 4-year old. They can just go on and on with their stories about their dog, what snack they had, which toy they picked, or what happened in the latest episode of Polar Bear and Friends. It can be rather boring, I know. And we usually just try to give our child the impression we are listening, when in fact we are thinking of a million other things. After they launch on a barrage of stories, we slowly tune out and attend to our own concerns. Don't worry, we all do it sometimes. Especially if we just come from a grueling day from work, it can be very difficult to listen.

But we have to know appropriate times when we have to use hearing and listening. Hearing is simply concerned with recognizing sounds. But listening entails giving your full attention to what is being said. If we just use our sense of hearing all of the time, we can miss out on certain important nuances our child may already be telling us. They may already be telling us important issues that make them feel sad or afraid. But because we are on autopilot mode, we fail to capture those details.

When we listen, we don't pay attention only to what is being said. We also have to recognize what is not being said. Sometimes, children's silence can be very telling. If you ask them "How was your day?" and they reply, "It's alright" but the tone is more somber or subdued than usual, then maybe we should probe some more. Certain clues like the tone of the voice, the body language, or the paucity of words may alert us to possible issues they may not be telling us. Listening is not just done with the ears. We all listen with our hearts, in fact, with our entire bodies.

There is a need to emphasize the skill of listening because we do it less than talking. There is a temptation to tell the child what to do, teach them what to say, or dictate how they should feel. Some of the traditionalists still hold on to the dictum "Children should be seen, not heard." The role of our children is to simply be passive receivers of our commands.

Subscribing to that thought can compromise your communication with your child. When you let your child speak, you are recognizing that they have something important to say. When you listen to them without cutting or interrupting their speech, you are conveying interest in their ideas. When you allow that precious silence to be filled by the child's account of events, you are acknowledging that they have a voice. Even if you expect them to say the same things over and over again, you still give them that opportunity to speak so they feel empowered. Even if you are smarter than them and that they may be telling things you already know, it matters to them that they are heard. They wouldn't crave so much attention if they know that their parents recognize their worth.

Don't be afraid to be silent with your kid. You don't need to always be doing or talking about something. Sometimes, your bond even becomes tighter when you are able to share quiet moments together. Your attitude towards listening and silence will be transmitted to your child. If they see their mom and dad appreciating silence at times, then they might practice it also. If they feel that they are being listened to, they will also feel that listening is something positive they can do. When both of you appreciate the value of listening to each other, then loud shouting matches can be avoided. You can command your child with a stare or a silent treatment. Silence is the seedbed where both parents and children can grow in communicating more effectively with each other.

Avoid Making Generalizations

When you are pointing to a particular behavior of your child that you want to stop, do not make generalizations about their actions. You have to stop saying words like "You are always like that" or "You are so stubborn all the time." We see this in Mollie when she told her son Jeremy "You are always playing tricks on your brother." When you generalize, you are showing just how much you don't pay attention to your child. They don't misbehave all the time, if you just bother to give them attention. Jeremy insisted that he didn't steal his brother's toy truck, but his mom did not believe it for a second. Maybe Jeremy was partly to be blamed for his persistent antics. But it did not help that the mother assumed that Jeremy misbehaved yet again. If we are always working on the assumption that children are going to behave badly, then they are more likely to misbehave.

The effect of generalizing can be traumatic to a child. If you generalize one misbehavior as a consistent character of the child, they may see themselves as bad people instead of focusing on the behavior. By using the word 'always,' you are telling them that they commit mistakes repeatedly and that they cannot change themselves. Children will feel that whatever good they do goes unnoticed. They react to this by misbehaving.

Instead of generalizing, be specific with what you want to say. Mollie could have made a better point if instead of saying "You are always playing pranks" she could have said "I caught you hiding your brother's toys three times this month already." The latter statement is more specific and can be verified. Jeremy would have to acknowledge this information because there were details to back it up. You are speaking of an observation, and not a judgment on their character. When you are correcting a misbehavior, you have to focus on the act and not on the person. Jeremy is lovable as he is, but his playing pranks on his brother is hurtful and should be stopped. You can only start correcting the particular behavior if you move away from generalizations that may seem unfair to your child.

You can only stop making generalizations if you place more attention on your child. You can zone in on specific behaviors you want to correct instead of attacking their person. Children will be very defensive and will not cooperate with you if you make sweeping claims about them. Notice not just the misbehaviors, but also their good behavior. "I noticed that you greeted Mrs. Robins this morning" or "I can see that you placed your crayons in the right box." These specific details will reinforce the good behavior you are noticing. We will discuss reinforcements with more in-depth details in the next chapter. But it is sufficient to say that behaviors that you want your child to continue should be noticed.

How Children Can Develop the Skill

When you are able to improve the quality of the attention you give to your children, you can now proceed to guiding your children to grow in their own attention skills. Sometimes, strong-willed children can be so impatient because they lack the ability to sustain attention on one objective or activity. A child may want this stuffed bear, and that musical box, and this truck and that robot, quickly shifting their interests when they see a lot of options. Or they can be so fixated on one obsession, determined to pursue it even if the situation is inappropriate or there are other equally good options available. A child might throw a tantrum if the parent did not buy the specific robot model, color, and dimension they want. These extremes in attention reflect the range of how children do poorly in attention. Here are some ways you can help your child develop a healthy sense of attention.

One Task At A Time

"Honey, could you take your toys, place it in a bag, clean your room, gather your dirty clothes in the corner and then do your homework." Sometimes, you may be having problems with compliance because your child is confused with multiple commands given at the same time. They refuse to follow you precisely because they don't understand which command to respond to first. For one-year-olds, they are only able to process one-step commands, while two-year-olds can do two-step commands. Older children can process more steps but our minds are only capable of processing so much information at the same time. If your boss told you to send out some emails, create a presentation, submit a report, take a few calls and make coffee all at once, you would also feel very confused. Imagine doing that to a child who has far less developed mental capacity to multitask.

Let your child finish one task at a time. It may take them a long time to accomplish it but there is much learning to be gained from focusing your attention on a singular goal. If you want them to clean the room, then they should not do anything else besides cleaning the room. There is a certain sense of satisfaction in having done one thing really well rather than doing many things half-heartedly and with poor quality. The child will appreciate it better if they are able to accomplish one task to the end rather than starting on multiple tasks which may not be completed.

Strong-willed children are also very impatient to move from task to task. They get irritated when they become stuck on one particular activity for far too long. If they are coloring a particular page for ten minutes already, they may want to flip the book and start on a new one. They end up starting a lot of activities which they don't finish. Poor performance in school often results from their eagerness to switch tasks and a tendency to be careless.

Help them grow in attention by giving them one activity at a time. Don't give them too many choices because they will want to try them all. Don't start another activity until you see that they have finished the previous. If they are going to color a page, they must make sure they finish the task before moving to another page. When you establish this rule, then children will be forced to focus on their particular task. They might notice certain details they may have missed. When they claim that they are finished, ask them questions. "Do you think you've covered everything?", "Are you satisfied with your work?" or "Would you like to recheck everything for a last time?" These prompts will help the child pay closer attention to their activity.

Limit Screen Time

The American Academy of Child and Adolescent Psychiatry (2020) conveyed that American children aged 8 to 12 years old spend an average of 4 to 6 hours of screen time every day, while teenagers spend up to 9 hours per day. Screen time included watching shows from television or on a gadget for hours on end. While these time periods may be normal for adults, exposing children to such a passive activity for these prolonged times is actually brain-deforming.

When you watch television, a limited number of circuits in the brain are engaged. I am not saying that watching television is a total waste of time. There is in fact a lot of good content on the Internet we can use to teach our children. The sense of sight and hearing may be stimulated as well as cortical areas associated with memory and emotions. But passive watching will stimulate only particular areas of the brain. The child merely receives information from their devices. The child cannot ask questions, use their own imagination, and engage in conversation when they just watch things on a screen. Brain only develops preferentially, with large areas for critical thinking unstimulated and undeveloped.

Compare watching television with actually playing with other children. In human interaction, the child is able to tap many parts of their brain. They can practice speech and conversation during face-to-face interaction. Without a visual stimulus, the child can develop their imagination when they read storybooks. Tactile stimulation gives the child much more information about texture, size, and shapes than watching two-dimensional figures. Real human interaction is indispensable to brain development.

We should also watch out for the content of the shows your child is consuming for 4 to 6 hours a day. There is so much material out there and children can be exposed to content that may not be suitable for them. Content like violence, risky behaviors, sex, substance abuse, fake news, and misinformation can all find their way into your child's devices. In older children, the issue of cyberbullying is very prominent, leading to increased levels of anxiety and depression among children and teenagers. As parents, we have the responsibility to filter the content we are exposing our children to. Parental controls are necessary to protect your child from unwanted and dangerous content.

The hidden danger in watching videos is that it is addicting. Children love to watch their favorite animal or cartoon shows because they are entertained. They laugh with the antics they see on television or sing along to nursery rhymes on the Internet. When the child is watching, the information from the screen stimulates reward areas in the brain that release endorphins which give them the feeling of happiness. So when that stimulus is taken away, the happiness also subsides. That is why children will insist on watching more and more content for longer hours because they are hooked to happiness. They get grumpy when you decide to cut their screen time. They feel agitated when they can't watch their favorite Fluffy Bear or toy review show. The addiction to entertainment and happiness deforms the brain. The attention skills of children are stymied because there is less active effort in the brain to analyze this information. The child ends up more impatient and short-tempered. What we construe as being strong-willed may in fact be repercussions of this addiction to entertainment on the screen.

Prolonged screen time can lead to problems in the different functional areas children engage in. A dip in the grades can be attributed to lack of extensive brain stimulation. As children watch longer, they are able to sleep less which makes them irritable. Because watching is a sedentary activity, weight gain and obesity develop from lack of exercise. The conversation and social skills are also deficient as the child becomes stuck with virtual and not actual human interaction. Anxiety is increased when the child compares the ideal world he sees on the screen with the real environment he is in. Body image becomes an important issue when girls compare themselves to the standards of what is considered beautiful in television.

Parents also use devices and the television to shirk off their parenting duties. If your son is throwing a tantrum, you calm him down by making him play video games. If you don't want your children running around the house, you hook them into their devices. These technologies become the substitute parents because it is convenient for us. With a screen turned on, we are able to focus on our other concerns aside from actually raising our children well.

As an adult, you have the sole responsibility of managing your child's screen time. You are the mother and the father of your child, not the screen. If you truly care about your child's development, then you should not relegate parenting to an inanimate technology. Left to themselves, children will watch and watch all day. They cannot help themselves. You have to be aware of how brain-deforming too much screen time and be more proactive in stimulating your child in creative ways. You have to monitor exactly what they watch and for how long. The American Academy of Child and Adolescent Psychiatry (AACAP) has recommended the following:

- Zero (0) screen time for babies until 18 months of age. The only exposure permitted is to talk with their parents who may be physically away from them and video calls are the only means of communication.

- From 18 to 24 months of age, the child can only watch educational programs with a caregiver. We have to note here that the purpose of watching at this age is not to entertain your child but to give them educational material such as learning nursery rhymes or identifying colors. Explore other forms of entertainment such as toys or playing games instead of watching a screen. The AACAP also recommended that the child should always be supervised by the adult. Yes, this is very inconvenient for us to watch children's programs while there are more practical things to do. But this is essential because your presence at this stage increases the affectionate bond between you and your child. You will also be able to control the content they are exposed to.

- For children aged 2 to 5 years, they may be allowed to watch non-educational shows for a maximum of 1 hour during weekdays and 3 hours during weekends. You have to be firm with these time schedules and make the rules clear with your child. If you set the rules straight in the beginning, they will bargain and whine less.

- For those aged 6 and above, you can give more leeway for their screen time. They may use the Internet for school activities or to relax. But still, you need to encourage them to adopt healthier habits like reading books, engaging in sports, or inviting their friends over.

During meal times, it may also be advisable to turn off all your gadgets. Dinner may be the only time that the family gets together at the end of the day. This rule should also apply to you. Even if you have urgent concerns, set a good example to your children by turning off your devices. Use the time to share stories or catch up with each other. A simple meal shared every day can actually increase your family's bond better than occasional holidays. When your children feel that your attention is undivided, they will feel important and appreciated.

When the children are about to sleep, do not place the gadgets in their bedroom. They will be sorely tempted to watch just a short 5-minute video when you are away. Before long, they couldn't sleep because they have become hooked on watching clip after clip. Take away that temptation and they will find it easier to sleep and rest their minds.

Chapter 5

Navigating Praise and Discipline

Rachel took her two girls to the grocery for their weekly supplies. This was their favorite bonding activity, with Tracy and Lisa helping to pick out items as Rachel pushed the cart. Rachel had a lot of items to cover since she was preparing for a big cook off this weekend.

"Tracy you can't put those candy jars on the cart. That's too much," chided Rachel. She knew the girls adored candy, but she knew they get too giddy and energetic when they have too much.

"But Mom, it's just one jar of candy. You let Lisa put in two bars of chocolate, but you won't let me put my jar of candy," pouted Tracy. She adored her little sister Lisa, but Tracy would sometimes feel that her mother gave in to Lisa's requests more often.

"It's ok to have those bars of chocolates. I think you'll like them too. But if you have too much candy, it's bad for your teeth. Let's go Tracy, we need to get to the next aisle."

"No, I want my jar of candy. If Lisa is going to have her chocolate, why can't I have my candy?" reasoned Tracy. Even though the chocolate was tempting, Tracy stood her ground. It wasn't fair and she was sticking to her request no matter what.

"I tell you what, none of you girls will have what you want. I'm sorry Lisa, but the chocolates got to go." Rachel returned the chocolates back in the sweets aisle and proceeded with the cold meats section. The girls were giving each other dagger looks, with Lisa silently accusing Tracy of ruining their sweet opportunity. Tracy made faces to spite her sister.

Rachel finished the rest of her shopping list in peace. The girls were particularly avoiding each other and Rachel felt guilty for causing the frosty divide. To make things up for her kids, Rachel says, "Alright you two.

You can each get an item you like that is not sweet. Just make it fast so we can go home early."

The girls were delighted with the sudden turn of events. They rushed to their favorite aisles, and quickly made their selection. When they came back, both were panting but were very excited with their finds.

"Ok girls what did you get?" Rachel said.

"Mom, this is the prettiest bow I have ever seen. And it comes in my favorite pink," gushed Lisa. She placed the bow in her hair to display just how pretty it is.

"Sure, place it in the cart," approved Rachel. "And Tracy what did you pick out?"

"Well, you said we could pick out anything that wasn't sweet, right? I chose this!" Tracy handed over a Nintendo Switch, sleek, shiny, and way too expensive.

Rachel balked at the price tag. "Honey, it's $350. I don't think it's time to buy a new console. This is too much."

"But Mom, you said we can pick anything we want that is not sweet. How come Lisa can get her bow and I can't have my console?" Tracy was starting to raise her voice.

"Well honey, the bow's considerably cheaper than your console. I'm sorry honey, but not this time."

Rachel placed the console on the top shelf where Tracy couldn't reach it.

"I want that console!" Tracy began to cry aloud.

"Well if you are going to behave like that, then neither of you will get what you want. If you want me to be fair, we won't buy Lisa's bow either." And with that, Rachel pushed her cart to the cashier, her two girls bawling their eyes out. Shopping was turning out to be Rachel's least favorite chore. Maybe, she won't bring along the girls next time.

Points for Reflection

- What are some methods you've tried to reward your children for good behavior?

- What are some ways you've tried to punish your children for misbehavior?

Why Praise and Discipline Matter?

You've come to this book primarily because you want to understand your child's strong-willed behavior. Perhaps you might even want to change it, especially those which you perceive to be harmful or inconvenient. The good news is that changing your child's behavior is possible. His being obstinate and disagreeable is not permanent and enduring. But it will not also go away on its own. How we raise our children can influence how these behaviors may persist or may abate. An understanding of how behavior is formed may be informative for us to gain some handle in managing our children.

Behavioral Theory

Behaviorism is a school of thought that subscribes to the idea that certain factors govern the formation, persistence, or diminishment of human behavior. Arguably the most influential of these behavioral theorists is BF Skinner. For Skinner (1976), human behavior is dependent upon and influenced on environmental factors from previous actions. What behaviors are continued or discontinued depend on the consequences of that behavior in the past. He calls this as *operant conditioning*. The person is conditioned to act in a particular way as a reaction to either reinforcement or punishment. The former refers to factors that lead to the persistence of a behavior, while the latter refers to factors that lead to the discontinuation of an action.

Four Types of Conditioning

Within the framework of operant conditioning, Skinner described four types of consequences. We will see how these can be applied in dealing with the behavior of strong-willed children.

Positive Reinforcement

When you want your child to continue a particular behavior, you provide them something they want or crave in exchange for doing that behavior. If you want your child to obey your command to clean his room, then you can reward them with a treat of cookies or extra hours of gadget use on weekends. As long as you reward them, their behavior persists. The problem with this type of conditioning is that when the reward (pizza) is gone, the desired behavior (cleaning the room) may also be discontinued.

Negative Reinforcement

When you want a desired behavior to persist, you take away something that the child dislikes. For example, you want your child to clean his room. By not nagging or taking away his gadgets, the parent can convince the child to clean his room. The desired behavior (cleaning the room) will only continue if the parent does not engage in the activity that the youngster dislikes (nagging).

Positive Punishment

If you want your child to stop a certain behavior, you provide a certain stimulus. For example, you want your child to stop throwing a tantrum by giving extra chores. Only as long as the father provides the stimulus (extra chores) will the unwanted behavior (tantrums) go away.

Negative Punishment

When you want your child to discontinue a certain behavior, you withdraw a certain stimulus. For example, you want your child to stop throwing a tantrum by grounding him from visiting his friends. The undesired behavior (tantrums) is discontinued for as long as the stimulus is absent (grounding).

Take some time to absorb these terms. It may take a while to understand what Skinner means by these different conditioning techniques. We may be more familiar with the terms 'rewards' and 'punishment' which we use with our children. If we want to reinforce a certain behavior, we provide certain rewards. If a child commits a behavior we do not desire, then we punish them. We need to use such methods strategically on children in order to influence their behavior.

How Parents Can Develop the Skill

Parents can devise creative ways of influencing their children's behaviors, some can be more effective than others. It can be a trial and error process of evaluating which method will work with any child. What is effective in one family may not be effective for another. Just because your neighbor uses grounding as a way of disciplining their child does not mean it will work for you. These strategies will only work in the situation in which you use them.

Make Clear Rules

In instilling discipline in your children, you must be able to lay down clear rules for your children. These rules are expectations of how they should behave. Not following those rules will mean certain consequences. Having definite rules in the house enables children to behave within certain limits. When you can put down clear rules that they can accept, it might be simpler to handle strong-willed children.

There are some characteristics of rules which make them effective in influencing behavior. You can try checking your own house rules if you are following these conventions:

Specific

Make sure that your rules are clear and specific. In the anecdote at the beginning of the chapter, we see how trouble erupts when Rachel makes vague rules which her girls misinterpret. "You can take whatever you want except for sweets." That could almost be anything. And Rachel punished her daughter when she brought an expensive gadget. It did fit her rule, but it was not what Rachel intended. The rule Rachel created was not specific enough causing various interpretations. Children are not lawyers who are out to spot loopholes in rules. They don't mean to break your rules. But you just have to make sure that your rules do not cause confusion.

Instead of using this rule......	You can use.....
Don't use gadgets too much.	No gadgets allowed in the bedroom. Use of gadgets allowed only for 1 hour on weekdays and 3 hours on weekends.
Take care of your things.	Return your toys in the boxes. Clean your shoes after going out.
Don't say dirty words.	Don't use curse words. Don't call your sister names.

You can make rules clearer by putting a time or a place marker. You may not be writing for a litigation case, but neither should you make vague rules.

Easy to Understand

Make rules that are easily understandable to children. Their vocabulary might be limited so don't overburden them with fancy words. It is good practice to consult your kids on how you should phrase the house rules. When kids take an active part in rule-making, they are easier to coax to follow. After all, they were there when the rules were made. If your kids can understand the rule, then everyone else can. Here are some examples of rules which are understandable for children:

Instead of using this rule...	You can use.....
Disinfect the plates.	Wash the plate after use.
Cap off your homework before booting up the television.	Finish your homework before watching television.
Push the old sack to the bins.	Take out the trash when it's full.

Reasonable

The most important aspect of a rule, whether it is for adults or for children, is that it is reasonable. If a rule makes sense, even your strong-willed child will recognize it. Rules are created to protect and safeguard the rights of people. For example, the rule "Brush your teeth before going to bed" protects the child's hygiene and oral health. Rules should not be used to serve random or personal interests. If you make a rule "No loud crying in the house," it might not make any sense at all. You can't prevent babies from crying nor should you prevent children from expressing their emotions. Don't make rules which will benefit you more than your children. This will be prone to comparisons and the children will complain. Create rules which truly protect your family's interests.

Take time to also explain the reason behind each rule. For example, your child may not understand why you have a rule like "Be home by 6 PM." They may reason out that they want to play outside beyond these hours. Instead of commanding your children to follow you because you are the parent, you can always refer to the reason behind the rule. An appeal to authority makes children want to disobey you all the more. Perhaps you can explain to them how being at home by night will protect them from dangers lurking in the dark, or that they need to rest at night. Don't tire of explaining to your kids the reason behind rules. Children find it harder to follow rules which were explained with "Just because I said so." They have a right to know why these rules are there.

Enforce Rules Consistently

If you create a rule, enforce them in a consistent manner and not just when you feel like it. The rule should apply to all. It would be unfair if you apply the rule to one child and not to the other. Siblings tend to compare how their parents treat them. Non-application of the rules to everyone will be prone to a lot of complaints, disobedience, and even fights between siblings.

Children are also looking up to their parents to follow the rules. If you make a rule of "No gadgets during meal time" and yet you bring one, then children will feel that it's fine to break the rules sometimes. If you really need to use your gadget, you can excuse yourself and take the call in another part of the house. Remember that you are modeling behavior to your children. They will imitate you on how you enforce and follow rules. You can win strong-willed children over by showing that you also follow the rules you've set. Rules are easier to follow when the adult shows the child he is also compliant.

Praise Good Behavior

The only times you may notice rules is when your children break them. When a child breaks your rule of "Don't play with the kitchen stove," you might immediately launch into a long dressing-down. It is good to catch misbehavior and tell your children off. But if misbehaviors are the only times you give your children attention, then it actually reinforces that behavior. A child might think "If playing with the kitchen stove will get Mom's attention, then I will repeat it." Strong-willed children often use this reasoning to justify their stubbornness. They may feel that their good behavior is often not noticed, while their mistakes are always highlighted. Instead of discontinuing the misbehavior, they will use it to catch the attention they crave from you. Don't you think it's the real concern if all you see in your child is a mistake?

Make an effort to notice more good things than what's wrong with your child. If your child was able to get by the week without eating sweets, praise them for it. If your daughter puts her dolls in the right place, commend her for it. If your son sleeps on time without arguing, tell him you appreciate it. These small gestures mean a lot to children. They will feel that the small things they do actually matter to you. Praise is a positive reinforcement used too infrequently by parents. But it is actually a powerful and empathic way of boosting a child's confidence and trust in themselves.

How Children Can Develop the Skill

When raising your children, it is important that you understand how powerful an influence you are as a parent. By using rewards or reinforcement and punishment, you may be able to develop good behaviors in your children. Parenting is not a means to control your children to act in ways you want them to. You are not enforcing rules or rewarding behavior because you want to dictate how exactly children should grow up to be. Rather, these strategies enable you to create an environment where your children can truly fulfill their potential. Caring for strong-willed children must come from a position of loving and not from a desire to dominate them. It should not be about your ego or seeing the child as a threat to your authority. When caring for strong-willed children, we want them to pursue the goals they want and to be the best person they can be, only by setting the right environment. Here are some ways you can use to help your child uphold the values of praise and discipline.

Make Children Appreciate the Value of Rules

Strong-willed children often rebel when they feel threatened by rules. They feel that rules are nothing more than commands which stifle their freedom. In their mind, they could ask questions like "Why do I have to clean my room?," "Why should I do my homework?" or "Why can't I eat more chocolates?" It's that never-ending series of 'whys' that annoy adults who may be too busy. But at the core of these inquiries is really the desire to know. Maybe children really want to know why and they haven't had a good explanation. As what we have explained earlier, make an effort to explain these rules to your child. If you believe that the rule is reasonable, it is just a matter of communicating that to your child. Once they are satisfied and can understand the reason behind rules, then following them becomes easier.

Take time out also to help your children appreciate how rules protect them rather than make them suffer unnecessarily. Children tend to focus on the restrictive properties of rules and how it causes them great inconvenience. But if you guide them into appreciating the greater positive value rules hold, then they will embrace these rules. It may only be a matter of communicating rules rather than disputing them.

Let Them Take Responsibilities

Give your child responsibilities in the house early on. For younger children, aged 2-3, you can invite them to put their clothes in the hamper, put their toys in the proper boxes, or pile their books in a corner. For those aged 4 to 5 years old, you can already ask them to make their beds, take out the weeds in the garden, clear the tables or empty the trash. For older children, they can be depended upon to wash the dishes, sweep the floor, make their own snacks, take care of the pet's needs, or fold the laundry.

When you involve children in doing household chores, you are empowering them tremendously. They will feel that they are important and that they contribute to the family. By being given responsibilities, the child feels a certain sense of control over his surroundings. It makes him appreciate rules more because now they are applying it in their everyday life. They don't need to grab power from you by being stubborn because they are able to express their agency and responsibility through these household chores.

As parents, don't expect that they will be perfect in doing the household chores. For sure, they will not sweep the floor completely or miss out on a few table stains while wiping the dinner table. They may not be able to fold their clothes in the standard you set or clean the rooms as you would have done. Assure them it's ok. The exercise of doing the household chores is of far greater value than doing things perfectly. They will grow into it with our guidance. Be patient with them and with yourself.

Boost Their Confidence

You can never be too generous with praising your child. Beneath the strong-willed child's resistance is an insecure kid just wanting to be noticed. You can break through that by being generous with your compliments. Commend them even for ordinary things that they did extraordinarily well. It may be as simple as making their beds or closing the door quietly. Your approval matters to them very much and they always find ways to seek it.

Commend efforts more than outputs. Your children are not perfect and they will make mistakes every now and then. Use these moments to teach them about the value of perseverance. If they did not get high grades this grading period, assure them that they can always try to be better on the next. If they weren't able to fold the clothes properly, you still have to compliment their efforts for helping out. Commending efforts help children relate well with failures and mistakes. It draws the child's attention to improving himself instead of wallowing in self-pity.

Finally, instead of fighting your strong-willed child's demands all the time, you can try to understand why they want to pursue a particular goal so much. It's easy to reject their insistence, but it's difficult to try to understand where they are coming from. Your daughter may insist on attending basketball clinics instead of the ballet classes you are pushing her to take. Instead of thinking about how obstinate and hard-headed she is, maybe you can ask her why she likes that particular sport instead. Perhaps she's insisting on playing basketball because she's passionate about it, rather than merely to spite you. Perhaps the label "strong-willed" isn't that awful after all if we pay more attention to our children. Apparently strong-willed children are just motivated children who are certain of their aspirations.

Chapter 6

Learning in Play

Christian invited his neighbor Shawn to play video games over their house during the weekend. Shawn was a regular in the house, and Dorothy generally approved her son's gesture of inviting friends over. Being an only child, Christian often played by himself. And Dorothy welcomed any chance they could invite someone over to play with her son.

"Good morning Mrs. Brown." Shawn respectfully greeted her. "Can I come in?"

"Sure you can." Dorothy liked Shawn particularly because he was polite. "Just go over to the living room and Christian is preparing your play stuff. Would you like an apple pie later?" Dorothy asked.

"Yes, ma'am!" Shawn exclaimed. He made his way eagerly into the living room. Christian has already finished setting up, and greeted his friend with their secret handshake. Before long, the two were already in the thick of their first game. They usually played racing games and they enjoyed competing with each other.

Christian took his games seriously. He was more competitive and hated losing. But Shawn was more of the laid back kind. He was a natural with games, effortlessly mastering any game after a few rounds. When he lost, he just shrugged it off. After two hours of playing, they were tied with ten games apiece. For the deciding round, Christian chose a sleek Lamborghini LP770 Alloy while Shawn chose a blue Porsche Taycan Turbo S. After just ten laps, Shawn won the game.

Christian slammed his controller on the ground. "That's not fair. You used the Porsche model. Of course you'll win if you use that car."

Shawn countered "Then you should have picked it. I won fair and square." He grinned to spite Christian.

Out of anger, Christian punched his friend on the cheek. Shawn was shocked, but retaliated quickly.

The two were at each other's throats, kicking, and punching until they fell to the ground.

Dorothy was in the middle of baking her famous pie when she heard the commotion. She rushed to the living room and was shocked to see her son and his best friend hissing and kicking each other. "Stop it you two," she commanded. The two desisted. "What happened here?" She demanded an explanation.

"Your son punched me because he thought I cheated. But I won fair and square ma'am." Shawn defended himself.

"No, Mom. He used a Porsche model and that gives him the advantage. He cheated by choosing that model." Christian replied, his cheeks throbbing red.

"I don't care about that game. You can play any game you want but I won't allow any violence in my house. Now who started the fight?" Shawn pointed at Christian who stood proudly, crossing his arms.

"Christian, say 'sorry' to your friend. I don't care if he cheated because you first punched him, you have to say 'sorry.' Do it now." Dorothy glared at her son.

"I don't want to. He cheated and I don't need to apologize for that." Christian said indignantly.

"That's no way to treat your friend. Nobody will want to play with you if you have that attitude." Dorothy pleaded with her son.

"Then I don't need friends who are cheaters." Christian stormed off to his room.

"I'm very sorry for the way my son behaved." Dorothy apologized to Shawn.

"Tell your mother that I take responsibility for my son and I will really discipline him this time. Would you like me to drive you home?" Dorothy asked. She knew she had a lot to explain to Shawn's mother.

"No problem, Mrs. Brown. Christian is like that even in class. He hates losing, that's why he doesn't have many friends. I just thought I would reach out." Shawn explained.

"Thank you very much, Shawn. You are a dear friend. I will have to talk to my son. But please don't hesitate to come back here anytime you want. You are always welcome to our house," offered Dorothy.

"Thank you ma'am. But I don't think I want to come any time soon. Maybe when Christian's better. Let's see. Bye, Mrs. Brown." Shawn went off.

Dorothy knew she had a lot to discuss with her son. Maybe there were unresolved issues she still didn't know about regarding her son's outbursts. She was concerned about her son's lack of social skills and pondered how she might best assist him.

Points for Reflection

What are your child's favorite games? In your time, what were some of the games you enjoyed playing? Do you remember playing any of these games?

- Hopscotch

- Four Square

- Marbles

- Red Light, Green Light

- Dodgeball

- Hide and Seek

- Capture the Flag

- Tag

- Jump Rope and Double Dutch

- Jacks

- Simon Says

- Bring Me

- Hand-clap games

- Musical Chairs

- Freeze Dance

- Basketball, Soccer or any other sports

Why Play Matters?

You might have recognized some of the aforesaid games or their variations in our time. But it's sad to know that most kids today don't even know these games. Instead, they might be more familiar with Super Mario, Pac-man, Minecraft, or Pokémon. I might not be too abreast with the latest video games but I'm sure video games are becoming more sophisticated year after year. It might not be fair to say that we had more fun during our time compared to today's generation with the games we played. But from a developmental perspective, games that do not involve videos and button-mashing will benefit your child's growth better.

As we have discovered in the last chapter, prolonged exposure to video games and television is brain deforming for the child. Although they are entertaining, these games are also addictive. The activity of play is essential to the development of a child. Play is the main activity for the two-to six-year-olds. It is a crucial time for them to develop cognitive, physical, and social skills. I strongly advocate that you should still expose your children to traditional games instead of predominantly video games or virtual interactions precisely because traditional games offer a holistic stimulus for growth. Among strong-willed children, their energy is more productively used in these traditional games rather than passive watching. The aggression is lessened and the child learns to be more cooperative and patient. We will discuss the many benefits of play and how they can temper the strong-willfulness of your child.

Cognitive Benefits of Play

Remember the games where you imagined cooking for your stuffed toys? Or when you pretended to be a doctor checking on a patient? These games may have been quite fun but they also expand your child's imagination far better than video games. Role-playing activities enable the child to expand their sense of imagination. In their minds, they can reimagine bed sheets to be the wardrobes of princes and princesses, a tree house to be a secret hideout, or a sandcastle for a magnificent palace. Compare this to watching a video which is a more passive activity. By just watching a video game, children are just sitting there, experiencing the creative world of the game producer instead of creating their own worlds.

When a child engages in role-playing games, they are also able to understand the social roles of a cook, a doctor, a firefighter, or a mechanic in an interactive and fun game. Children enjoy it when they dress up as a mailman, a mermaid or even as a character from a storybook. There is a simplistic awareness of how society functions when they interact with dolls or play house. In a subtle way, play helps children make sense of their existing culture, understand the hidden rules of social interaction and vicariously experience the life of other people.

Play breaks the fixation of the strong-willed child on a singular goal. The beauty of play is that there is much room for spontaneity and improvisation, even if there are certain rules. In basketball for example, there are certain rules like getting a score only by shooting the ball in the basket or staying only in a specific play area. But you can never predict how each game will play out. No game is exactly the same as others. This is quite unnerving for children who are fixated with rituals or certain patterns of behavior. Play is very spontaneous and can break the rigidness of your strong-willed child.

Physical Benefits of Play

Play is also a very physical activity. Jumping ropes can be exhaustive. Hopscotch involves much hand-eye coordination. Playing marbles engages your fine-motor movements. The physicality of games improves the gross and fine motor development of children. In fact, developmental pediatricians look at milestones in play to check if a child is growing normally. At one year old, a child must be able to stand by himself. A two, he should be walking and running. At three, he should be able to navigate stairs. At four, the child must display the ability to hop on one foot. Rapid motor development is expected from children aged two to six years old. Failure to stimulate physical activity may lead to weakness in muscle movements.

The physicality of play also exhausts the aggression and other intense energies a strong-willed child may be experiencing. The child can sublimate his frustration by kicking a ball during a soccer game. Girls can use their pent-up energies as they proceed in increasing difficulties of Double Dutch. After an exhaustive game, children will be too tired to throw a tantrum or insist on a demand. The energy they feel becomes translated to something productive when they engage in play. Physical activity releases happy hormones that reward the child for the effort. They may be tired, but they enjoyed every minute of playing.

We can greatly appreciate this when we compare traditional games with video games. In the latter, children can remain in a particular position for prolonged periods of time. The only muscles working while playing video games are the eyes and the fine-motor movements of the hands. But children feel more aggressive and anxious because they have a lot of excess energy that is unused in playing video games. Obesity and poor nutrition are the results of this sedentary lifestyle. Diseases like hypertension, hypercholesterolemia or diabetes which are more observed in adults may develop prematurely as children exercise less and consume less nutritious food.

Social Benefits of Play

Games are also played with other children. While you can play video games alone, it is impossible to enjoy Double Dutch by yourself. Essential social skills are developed exclusively in physical games. Playing with other children will let your child increase in their empathy because they are exposed to other people's emotions and concerns.

Cooperation is developed in games. The concept of a team relies heavily on the ability of children to set aside their personal agenda in order to achieve a collective goal. Sports are very good in forming a cooperative bond among children. You want to win, but you can only succeed by working with other people. This means you have to compromise and learn to delegate tasks to other people. In a game of soccer, a strong-willed child may want to be the one kicking the ball all the time. But because he is playing with other children, he must pass the ball to others who may be in a better position to score a goal.

Interacting with other children will also show your child the consequences of actions. Fights are normal during games and are actually formative. When somebody pushes another player, the victim will try to retaliate. This is then an opportunity for the child to learn how his action triggers emotions in the other person and how this can lead to certain behaviors. Children learn emotions and the consequences of actions as they are playing. This allows your strong-willed child to go beyond his self-centered interests into an appreciation that other children also have their emotions. Play breaks the strong-willed child's stubbornness, giving way to compromise.

Play can also bring about the competitive spirit of children. We all want to win and we want to defeat others. Competition is good because it forces your child to perform their very best, to push their personal boundaries. Winning a game rewards the child's efforts and reinforces the value of excellence and grit. But losing is also a good formative tool for children. There may be objective winners and losers in play, but simply engaging in the activity already makes every child a winner.

This multi-dimensionality of play makes it a central formative activity in children. When you allow your child to play especially physical games with other children, you are strengthening their cognitive, physical, and social development. If you condone their addiction to video games, then they are cutting all these different dimensions from being fully developed. In play, the strong-willed child becomes someone who is cooperative, competitive, and empathic.

How Parents Can Develop the Skill

You might think that your role as parents is just to cheer your children on during games or to bring in the treats after an exhaustive match. But I actually invite you to engage in active play with your kids. Yes, even parents should spend time playing with their kids. The goal in playing with your kids is obviously not for you to win, but to increase your affectionate bond with your children. Playing games can also be an opportunity for you to teach important life skills in an enjoyable context.

Let Children Lead

Strong-willed children resent being told what to do. They refuse to follow commands because they are always at the receiving end of it. Unknowingly, we may even be influencing what children should enjoy by buying the kinds of toys we think they will enjoy. We tell our children which games to play, what drawings to make, or which books to read. In subtle ways, we are trying to control them even when we don't mean to. Thus, their stubbornness is their way of telling us that they resent being controlled.

Play gives you that wonderful opportunity to let your children lead. Since play is primarily for children to enjoy, let your child choose what games they want to play or what activity they want to engage in. Consciously guard yourself from exerting undue pressure on them, as you do in other aspects of their life. You can consider the following statements as you play with your child.

Instead of saying...	You can say...
Let's draw a house.	What would you like to draw?
That looks like a tower you are building.	What are you building?
I will be the patient.	Which role would you like to play? The doctor or the patient?
This doll looks pretty. Should we buy this?	What would you like to buy?
You should color the frog green.	That's an interesting color for a frog.
This Lego princess should be placed in the castle.	Where should we place this?
I think you enjoyed the game.	What did you feel?

As shown in the table, most of the statements in the left column are commanding statements. They point to a particular direction or suggest a particular interpretation. When you say this to your child, you expect them to just agree with you. The statements don't invite participation from the child, but seem like commands needed to be followed. When they don't agree with your opinion or refuse your command, you label them as stubborn or too strong-willed. What if they really don't want to draw a house? What if they don't want that doll you are suggesting? The statements in the left column are not helpful in making your child appreciate themselves.

The last left-hand statement is particularly important. When you say "I think you enjoyed the game," you are dictating what the child should be feeling. This could be another form of gaslighting, when you use your authority to dictate the emotions of others. Gaslighting involves making other people question their own thoughts and emotions to forward your own. Children have their own emotions which are just as important as yours. The same activity can impact you differently. So it may not be helpful for you to suggest emotions your child should be experiencing.

The right-hand column presents a good statement you can use when engaging your child in play. All of the statements are in question format. By phrasing it as a question, you are inviting the child to respond. It veers away from a position of authority and command to a position of an inquisitive friend. The statements are very open-ended and allow your child to take control of the situation. Even if in reality, frogs are supposed to be green, allowing your child to use a different color enables them to expand their imagination. Instead of dictating their emotions, you are allowing them to share their own feelings. This gesture makes children feel that they are important and that their feelings are valid and valued.

You will always be the adult and for most of the time, you will be making decisions for your child. But when you play with them, allow your child to have that sense of control. Stimulate their imagination and respect their feelings about the situation. When you allow these pockets of control, the strong-willed child will be more secure and less prone to grab power from you. When their feelings are acknowledged, they will not feel the need to hoard attention by throwing a tantrum. Make your child feel more confident and secure about their decisions, starting with non-threatening activities like play.

Enjoy Your Time

Another tendency we need to unlearn is to 'overteach.' As parents, we feel obliged to always impart a lesson or to teach our kids a life skill. But the position of teaching is still a position of power and authority. It always assumes that the adult is in command and has the monopoly of information. Again, the strong-willed child resents this notion. They are appreciative of learning, but they also resent always feeling powerless themselves to teach. You can empower your child by removing that teaching hat and shift towards being a friend or even being a student. Allow your child to feel that he has something good he can teach you.

While playing, give yourself a chance to also enjoy. Maybe for adults, the enjoyment does not come from winning or losing a game. The pleasure comes from being able to bond with your child. Laugh when you make mistakes. Tease and cajole to get a reaction. Let the child win, sometimes. Playing with your child should also make you a child. Games bring about a certain pleasure in the sheer spontaneity of the moment shared by people who genuinely love each other.

When your child sees that you are enjoying yourself, they will feel a deeper connection with you. If you show them that it's fine to lose, then they will feel better about it. If you laugh out loud, then it informs the child that it is okay to express happiness in an exuberant way. Even without consciously teaching, you are helping your child enjoy learning emotions.

Document these precious moments with your child. Take pictures, keep their toys and store their letters. Your children will grow up very fast and you won't be able to play as many games with them as before. Past the school ages, teenagers would rather bond with their peers than with their parents. It is natural. So before they grow up too fast, take these moments when you can enjoy their childhood. When strong-willed children have good memories with their parents, they feel more secure and less likely to antagonize them.

How Children Can Develop the Skill

Strong-willed children are very intuitive and quick to learn. Their strength lies in being self-reliant. So let them learn as much as they can in the activity of play. Give them the opportunity to learn from their friends about cooperation and competition. Allow them to play and get hurt sometimes. Our role as parents is to create opportunities where they can grow. Instead of dictating what they should be learning, we have to trust that our children are capable of adapting to situations quickly. We can be of more use to them when we try to process their feelings and learnings. The experience of play is going to bring a lot of new insights and feelings from our children. By listening more and teaching less, we can be more effective parents. Here are some important lessons you can lead them to realize:

Establishing Friendships

What's wonderful in letting children play with other children is that their perspectives expand from an ego-centric view to a recognition of the other. In social interactions, the child realizes that there are other people of their age who have their own emotions and thoughts. And these could be totally different from the child's. Because they are equal, the child sees the playmate not as an authority figure who will make commands. The other kid is like himself, but different. The encounter with the other kid becomes an opportunity to learn other perspectives, emotions, and thoughts which are from an equal and not from somebody superior. They both become curious about each other, as they discover similarities and differences.

At the heart of all human encounters is that recognition of sameness. That stranger becomes a friend because we recognize something that we share in common. It may be because you have similar interests or you live in the same area. You may have gone to the same school, sat beside each other, or shared a similar experience, that is why you became friends. The start of any friendship lies in identifying a common ground. This is not something we can teach our children. It is something they must learn by themselves. All we need to do is provide opportunities for them to encounter other people and to establish their own friendships.

And for parents, we want to encourage these friendships for our children. We want them to find their own sets of friends who they can learn from and enjoy with. We may not be able to dictate who their friends should be, but we can be supportive by feeling positive for our child. For a strong-willed child, having friends will make them less combative of parental authority. Their energies are poured out to enrich these relationships rather than resisting authority.

Compromise

We have seen how games help children work in teams. Children learn to work with each other to achieve a common goal. They set aside differences so that they can win a game or defeat an opponent. Team sports foster that camaraderie among children. Part of teamwork is compromise. As a member of a team, a child gives up certain interests for a suitable exchange. The goalie of a soccer team gives up his desire to score a goal in order to help the team by preventing the other team from scoring. In jumping ropes, you wait your turn before you can play. You endure flipping the ropes for other people as they complete their jumps. And when it is your turn, you get to enjoy skipping as the other player flips the rope. Compromise is a valuable skill for children to learn. You will not always get what you want when you work in a team. But in exchanging certain interests, you aspire to gain much more than what you gave away.

We can also apply this in the parent-child relationship. In a family, you are in the same team, working towards the same goal. As much as we want our children to follow our commands, we also have to respect that they may have their own interests. You can soften your strong-willed child if as a parent, you are also willing to compromise. If you shift from an authority figure to a teammate, then the child will be more amenable to cooperate with you.

For example your child insists on going to the park at this moment. Your five-year old kid is throwing a tantrum, demanding that you should take him to the park to play. What will you do?

1. Ignore the kid's tantrums and let him kick about until he gets tired.

2. Take him to the park to stop the tantrums.

In the first option, you are bending the child to your will. You are insisting on your authority and neglecting the child's concerns. In the second, you relinquish your power and follow your child's demands. It calms the child down but you can be abused the next time. The child realizes that he can control you if he uses tantrums.

Either of these options lead to less optimal outcomes. The first option will make the child resentful and feel neglected. The second diminishes your authority and opens you to being vulnerable to your child. A better solution then is to also practice compromise yourself. If you are willing to compromise, then your child may also be open to that possibility too. In compromise, you can offer the following suggestions:

- We will go to the park, but not now. Mommy is busy at the moment and we can visit the park during the weekends instead.

- We will go to the park only after we have cleaned your room.

- We will not go to the park, but you can have 30 extra minutes of television instead.

By opening these possibilities, you can expand your child's perspective about the situation. When you compromise, you make the child part of your team, acknowledging their importance. You will only antagonize them more if they feel that they are always powerless with you. There are situations wherein you cannot totally meet halfway. But the mere attempt to compromise will be greatly appreciated.

It's OK to Lose

Nobody likes to lose. When you play a game, you play to win. Defeat means you are weak or deficient in some way, as compared to the winner. There is a sense of shame and disappointment, a loss of self-esteem and confidence. Nobody wants to hang around with losers. The ego is severely bruised when you are defeated.

This makes the strong-willed child very vulnerable to a negative idea of defeat. They are stubborn and inflexible, because they are confident about their abilities. But when they experience defeat, the focus shifts to the ego. In the case of Christian at the beginning of this chapter, he cannot accept that he lost to his friend Shawn. Christian deemed himself highly with his hand and eye coordination skills. But when somebody disproved that, Christian interpreted that as an attack against his person. Strong-willed children are sore losers because they are very protective of their ego.

We can help our strong-willed children cope with defeat by guiding them towards rethinking about their perspective on losing. Instead of being ashamed, we can guide them into taking defeat as a teacher. Maybe Christian's mother could talk to him about his feelings and thoughts about losing. It is perfectly valid to feel bad about losing. Yes, there is that sense of sadness and disappointment. But losing also teaches us that we are not perfect and that there is room to improve. Maybe Christian could practice more so he could be better next time. Or maybe Shawn was just lucky and Christian wasn't. There is always a second chance to try again.

Losing also reveals what is important to us. Is winning the game more important than being kind to a friend? Should we win at all costs even if it means hurting another person? You can always use defeat as a teaching moment for your kids to learn about being humble in losing and happy for the success of others. They will be able to practice this if they also see us graciously accepting our own defeats. We are better able to connect to our strong-willed children when they are most vulnerable in defeat.

Chapter 7

Managing Your Emotions

"Daddy let's go home," Harper said for the nth time. They were waiting in line for the dentist and this Saturday seemed quite slow.

"It's ok bud. You're up for a while, just wait for your turn, you'll get your teeth cleaned too." Jacob said while checking out his phone. They had booked their dentist appointment only the night before. It was a miracle they were even accommodated in the schedule.

"But dad, I don't want to wait in line. I think we are wasting our time here. I can just go home and play my console instead," whined Harper.

"Well, we're not going home until you have your teeth checked. You've been complaining about that tooth pain for weeks and a little more waiting shouldn't matter. Go find something to busy yourself with," Jacob said. It was lucky he was also free to take his child out to the dentist this weekend. Normally, his schedule would be so packed. Jacob thought he needed to take the time out to be with his son. But waiting in line was as inconvenient for him as it was for Harper.

"Maybe we can ask the other kids if we can go first. I don't think they'll mind," suggested Harper.

"Do you have somewhere else you need to be Harper? Why the rush, son? You'll get your teeth checked in no time," Jacob replied while browsing through his calendar. The next week seemed packed with meetings and he wasn't looking forward to that.

They sat in the common area together with the other patients. Harper was always looking at the door, hoping that his turn would come up. He kept fiddling his hands and tapping his feet on the ground to ease his tension.

"We have been here for almost thirty minutes dad, I think we should just reschedule." Harper was getting impatient.

"No Harper, we're getting your teeth checked even if it takes us the whole day. Just be patient and you will get in there in no time." Jacob said exasperatedly.

"But I don't want to wait anymore. I want to go home." Harper started to make a scene collapsing on the ground and throwing fits. The other children and parents just stared at him.

Jacob felt the heat rush into his head. "Harper, stop it this instant. You're making a scene. You're a big boy now and you can wait for your turn."

"I don't want to. Home, home, home, I want to go home!" Harper shouted.

"Tell you what, if you stop that at this instant and we wait for another thirty minutes, I will buy you your favorite ice-cream you want. Remember that chocolate sundae topped with nuts and marshmallows you like? I'll order you two servings of that if you behave," bribed Jacob.

For a moment, Harper was arrested in his fits. He thought about the proposition. "Does that come with sprinkles and wafers?" He asked.

"All the sprinkles and wafers you want, we'll order. Just get off the floor now and sit like the grown up boy you are," continued Jacob.

Harper looked at his father suspiciously. The ice-cream certainly sounded tempting. But the line was also pretty long. There were around five kids still ahead of them and Harper didn't want to wait any longer.

"No, let's go home," and he continued thrashing around on the floor.

Mouthing a "sorry" to everyone, Jacob took his thrashing son and carried him out of the dentist's clinic. It took a while for Harper to calm down. Jacob dejectedly drove home, feeling defeated yet again by his small boy.

"You won't have that delicious ice-cream, I'll make sure of that." He shouted at Harper.

The two didn't speak to each other during the rest of their way home.

Points for Reflection

Which of these emotions can you relate the most to?

- Calm

- Peaceful

- Contented

- Joy

- Bliss

- Ecstatic

- Exuberant

- Gleeful

- Delirious

- Amused

- Interested

- Grateful

- Enraptured

- Confident

- Enthusiastic

- Jovial

Why Managing Your Emotions Matters?

The last pillar of the empathic framework focuses on managing emotions. We have touched briefly on the importance of feelings and emotions in the previous chapters. But it deserves a more in-depth discussion because it is often neglected by parents. Much of the problems we experience in dealing with strong-willed children stem from the different negative emotions they display. Strong-willed children display emotions like frustration, anger, anxiety, and impatience in such intense and dramatic ways. The yelling, kicking, punching, and crying externalized the tension they must be feeling inside. In order to help our children understand themselves better, perhaps we should also revisit what we know about emotions.

What Are Emotions?

Hockenbury and Hockenbury (2007) described emotions to be complex psychological states individuals experience in reaction to external stimuli. They described emotions to have three distinct components: the subjective experience, the physiological response, and the behavioral manifestation.

Subjective Experience

Our feelings are subjectively experienced. We can describe our feelings to other people, but they cannot feel the exact emotion we are experiencing at that moment. In the exercise at the beginning of this chapter, all of the emotions mentioned are related to the general feeling of 'happiness.' The feeling of being calm, contented, amused, and ecstatic may all refer to someone who is happy. But the use of different words show how complex that feeling is. There is a range in the degree of happiness. They all refer to happiness, but to varying degrees of it.

It may happen that we are only feeling one emotion at a time. For example, if you were left by the bus, you would feel frustrated. Or if you receive a gift, you feel jubilant. But there are also times when you can feel more than one emotion. Different emotions, some more dominant than others, can co-exist in any time period. Using the previous examples, imagine that you were left by the bus. While you feel frustrated, you may also feel disappointed at yourself for waking up late. Sometimes, these emotions can even be conflicting with each other. For example, imagine that you receive a gift. You may feel happy about such a surprise. But you can also feel sad at the same time if you discover that it's not the gift you were expecting. We may feel a mix of emotions happening at the same time.

Physiological Response

A bodily reaction accompanies the subjective experience of emotion. When you feel excited, your heart beats faster, your palms become sweaty and you feel butterflies in your stomach. What we experience cognitively in the brain translates to physiological changes.

Strangely enough, the similar physiological responses can occur from different emotions. The heart beating faster, the palms sweating and butterflies in the stomach can also illustrate a person who is afraid or nervous. It may be difficult to identify the emotion just by looking at the physiological response.

Behavioral Manifestation

The final component of emotions is the external or behavioral manifestation. The emotion is communicated to other people in various ways. You may have an idea of what a person is feeling just by looking at their facial expression, the body language, or the tone of the voice. When you look at a person with a glum face, you may guess that he is feeling sad. When a student is called to recite in front of the class, the stammering and the shaking of the body tell you that he may be nervous about the ordeal.

Some people are able to mask the behavioral manifestation of their internal emotion. Actors often portray emotions which are different from their real feelings. They may be playing the role of a jester making people laugh. But in reality, they may be feeling the opposite. We can fake a feeling if we want to.

Taken together, the subjective experience, physiological response, and the behavioral manifestation describe the total experience of a feeling. All of us have feelings, whether we manifest it outwardly or fake it completely. We experience feelings as a reaction to an external event. You don't just feel happy without any reason. Perhaps you passed a test or your crush waves at you. Our feelings are very dependent on the events happening around us. Feelings enable us to survive. When we feel afraid, we run from a perceived danger. When we are hungry, we are moved to look for food. There is great value to our feelings.

Different psychologists suggested a differing number of basic human emotions. Paul Eckhman (2005) described six universal categories of emotions: happiness, sadness, anger, fear, surprise, and disgust. They are universal, cutting across cultures. Though there are variations in expression, emotions can be understood by everyone. For example, a picture of a boy smiling can be interpreted by anyone as showing the feeling of happiness. As we have seen in the exercise, within each basic emotion, there are differing degrees and intensities. You can be somber, unhappy and depressed, all of them related to sadness but to differing degrees.

This knowledge of emotions is important for us parents to understand ourselves and our strong-willed children. Emotions have a tremendous impact on behavior. In every episode of tantrums or stubbornness, there is an underlying feeling we need to recognize, understand, and value.

How Parents Can Develop the Skill

Before we can teach our children about emotions, we also have to understand how feelings also affect us personally. When the adult does not even understand his or her feelings, how can they relate and understand the feelings of their children? The following skills are essential for you to discover and manage your own feelings.

Recognize and Identify Your Own Emotions

When your child throws tantrums, the tendency is to focus our attention on the act and on the child. We recognize that they are frustrated or even angry at us. But we also have to recognize that we are also triggered by the actions of our children. When they punch or kick us, we feel angry as well. When our commands are not being followed, we are enraged.

When our child whines constantly, we feel irritated. Recognizing our own feelings is the first step towards controlling them.

Naming feelings is another skill which we take for granted as adults. When somebody asks "How are you?", we instinctively reply "I'm OK." Being "OK' is not a feeling. Saying that you are "OK" is a lazy effort to actually think about what you are feeling. "OK" does not fall in any of the basic emotions Eckhman proposed.

Controlling your emotion depends on your ability to name what you are feeling. Find the right word to the emotion you are experiencing as you witness your child thrashing about. Are you annoyed or bothered? Are you disappointed or frustrated? Are you enraged or murderous? Aside from anger, are you feeling other emotions? These questions are necessary for us to answer if we want to conquer our feelings. We also want to teach our children how to name their own feelings so they can control them. Practice it first yourself.

Think Before You Act

Our emotions are so powerful that they can influence our behavior. Sometimes, the translation can be very instinctive. After being punched, you feel angry and you punch back at the other person instinctively.

When somebody grabs your hair, you reflexively grab back in retaliation. Emotions are powerful drivers of behavior.

The problem with reactive behavior is that it often leads to less than optimal outcomes. In your anger, you can make decisions which you might regret later on. You feel so angry about your child's defiance and you instinctively smack him hard. Other people even commit acts far worse than just smacking. Afterwards, you feel sorry about your actions. But you can't erase that event from your child's memory anymore. Your emotions have caused you to commit actions which can further exacerbate an existing problem.

And so, always think before you act. Recognize that you have feelings, that you are angry and hurt by your child's stubbornness. But moderate your feelings with your critical thinking. Ask yourself, "What is the best course of action?" or "Will my action solve the problem?" You cannot always say that you were triggered by your child to hurt them back. We are adults capable of thinking and controlling our emotions. We cannot let our own emotions control us. Your actions will trigger a downstream consequence. Your child hurts you, and you hurt them back. They become angry with you, and your anger increases. It's a never-ending cycle of reactive behaviors. You are an adult, fully capable of managing your own emotions. Before you can help the child manage their own feelings, you must also control yours first.

Breathe

When things become very intense, it is good to pause and breathe before doing anything. Breathing serves a number of useful purposes in mediating emotions. First, when you breathe, you are replenishing your body with needed oxygen which has been depleted by the stressful event. When you have more oxygen in your brain, you are able to think better about your situation and your next decisions.

Next, breathing allows you to cut the instinctive arc of emotions to behavior. Some people count slowly from one to ten while concentrating on their breathing when they feel angry. The delay from emotion to action helps you calm down and think clearer. You want to stop yourself before you let anger take over you. By concentrating on breathing, you are diverting your attention away from the stressful event into a calming activity.

Finally, breathing reduces your stress levels. It can lower your blood pressure by making you more relaxed. It alleviates any physical or psychological pain as your body shifts to healing itself. When you concentrate on your breathing, the tension in your body is lifted. In this relaxed state, you are more able to make good decisions for you and your child.

So the next time your strong-willed child annoys or angers you, just concentrate on your breathing. Let your calmness soothe the frustration they feel. They are expecting you to be angry. If you show them calmness, their intense emotions will also subside. When you speak more slowly and deliberately, they will also feel the need to imitate your behavior. Your sense of peace in the middle of conflict will rub off on your children.

How Children Can Develop the Skill

It is very difficult to teach children about their emotions. The ability to reflect and control emotions develops slowly and gradually. Higher cortical centers in the brain need to be more developed before a child can reflect about their own mental and emotional processes. Be patient in teaching kids about emotion because they will not understand it right away. It is essential that you start this process even at a young age. Reading social cues and practicing empathy will allow your strong-willed child to momentarily detach from their concerns into recognizing the feelings and emotions of other people.

Recognize and Identify Their Emotions

Teaching kids to recognize and identify their feelings is quite challenging. Their emotions can be so intense and overwhelming they may not have the right words to express their internal experience. They may not have enough mental resources to think before they act. It is our duty as parents to guide them in managing their own emotions.

In the beginning of the chapter, we see Harper losing his temper while waiting in line. He felt so anxious and impatient for being made to wait. When his father refused to take him home, his anger overwhelmed him and he burst into a tantrum. How can his father help him to understand his emotions?

In conducting a conversation with your child about emotions, it is not helpful to assume what they are feeling. You can start by focusing on the behavior they exhibited and ask them the emotion behind their behavior.

For example, Jacob could open the conversation with "Harper, you were throwing a tantrum when I refused to take you home. What were you feeling?"

This statement and the following question invite the child to identify his own feelings. This is important. It might already be obvious to you what they are feeling. But the exercise is really for them to verbalize what their internal experience is. Don't assume what children are feeling. Let them speak and describe their feelings in their own words.

As children, their vocabulary may be limited. They are still growing in their understanding of words. They may not yet know the subtle differences between being annoyed or being infuriated. They may just feel angry. Teach them the names of specific emotions. The more that they can name feelings, the more they can control them. If they do not know the name of what they are feeling, they cannot manage it completely.

Understanding Consequences

From recognizing and identifying feelings, you can lead your child to discover the relations between emotions and behavior. The child must understand how their emotions become translated to actions. We cannot make that connection for them. We can only lead them to an understanding of that relationship.

For example, Jacob can say "Ok, so Harper, you felt very angry at me. So because you were angry, what did you do?"

In this example, Jacob already knew the answer to his question. But he is leading Harper to make the connection between his anger and his throwing a tantrum. If you just tell the child the connection right away, he may not retain that relationship well. Let your child think for himself.

Next, lead your child to understand the consequences of his actions. The strong-willed child only focuses on his emotions and his personal concerns. When you draw further connections between his action to succeeding consequences, the child begins to have an understanding about the impact of his singular action.

For example, the conversation could play out as:

Jacob: So Harper, now that we are home because you threw a tantrum, what will happen to your teeth?

Harper: They won't be checked by the dentist.

Jacob: And if they are not checked by the dentist, what will happen?

Harper: My teeth will hurt more.

This is a very simplistic reenaction but it demonstrates how we can lead the child to understanding the consequences of his action. Harper might think twice again if he will throw a tantrum knowing that his teeth might hurt more. Children might not be able to think more than two or three steps ahead of their actions. Just guide them gently through this process.

Explore Possibilities

Finally, we can guide the child into exploring other ways they can express their feelings knowing the consequences of their action. Strong-willed children can only think of one way to reach their goal. For example, Harper can only think of throwing a tantrum to get his wish not to prolong his waiting in line. But there are other ways to get to the goal besides the more destructive and stressful method Harper chose to respond. Our goal as parents is not to think of these alternative ways. Our goal is to guide our children to think about other possibilities of achieving their goal in life-giving ways.

For example, Jacob could ask "Harper, aside from going home by throwing a tantrum, can you think of other ways which will help you be less anxious in waiting in line?"

In this statement, Jacob is inviting his son to solve his anxiety problem by generating many solutions. The more possibilities Harper can generate, the more options he can choose from to deal with the situation. These possibilities include:

- Reading a book so he can pass the time

- Draw in his sketchpad so he doesn't get bored

- Playing with a video console to feel less anxious

-

Sharing stories with his father to divert his attention from the long line

- Ask other people politely if he could go ahead

If you just allow your child to generate possibilities, you will be surprised at how creative they can be. The next time they encounter a problem, the child is more equipped with choices on how to react to the situation. They may not choose to be strong-willed and stubborn if they recognize other more effective and mature ways of dealing with the situation.

Conclusion

I visited my sister's family some years back and I had an interesting encounter. As I was entering the house, I was surprised to see my niece, Vanessa, slumped in one corner, wailing loudly. She was so inconsolable. I went up to her and asked "Vanessa why are you crying? Is there anything wrong?" I thought for a moment that she might have tripped or hit something hard, given the intensity of her crying. Between sobs, she managed to say, "Mommy says I can't have more chocolate cake. I want more cake!" She was so cute, sitting there, crying aloud, and looking for cake.

Having met a lot of strong-willed children, I have noticed one thing in common with all of them:

they are all very intense. Strong-willed children refuse commands intensely, cry loudly, and throw a tantrum dramatically. They have remarkable energy levels, tiring out their pleading, bargaining or even threatening parents. If they have a goal no matter how trivial, they are going to fight for it, tooth and nail. Even for another slice of chocolate cake, Vanessa would be crying as if it was the end of the world.

I feel very much for all parents out there struggling to take care of children who are very strong-willed. These children can really get into your nerves, with their unreasonableness and stubbornness. I understand if sometimes, you are at your wit's end and burst from the stress they can cause you. With so many other concerns in life, you would expect your children to at least cooperate. I understand if there are more times that you don't understand your child and how they can be so illogically obstinate.

But I feel so much more for strong-willed children unable to harness that intense energy they feel inside. The frustration, anger or anxiety they feel inside becomes bottled up, reaching a limit until they just burst. They may not have the right words to express what they are feeling, nor do they know other ways of venting out their energies.

In these trying situations, choose to be calm. It won't do any of you good if you fight fire with fire. Do not rush to drastic actions which you may regret. Let your calmness soothe the fire of your child. Let calmness enlighten you to see the situation with a greater perspective and enable you to make better decisions.

In these trying situations, choose to understand. As an adult, you have greater mental resources to cope with stress. You must be able to manage your own emotions and try to understand where your child may be coming from. Your child may be coming from a position of hurt and anxiety. Set aside your own ego and try to broaden your perspective.

Choose to love more in these tough situations. The intensity of your child's emotions reflects their ability to love strongly as well. Channel those energies into something life-giving. Act with love and not in anger or irritation. It may be difficult, but remind yourself to always love more. After all, no matter how stubborn, unreasonable, and whiny your children are, they are still your children. Love begets love. So choose to love more.

Leaving a Review

As a self-published author, I find it important not only to write great books but also provide my readers with the best value possible. Being an Indie writer means I don't have access to all the perks of a traditional publisher, such as a publicist to get the word out about my latest releases. That's where you come in. A little bit of your time can go a long way towards helping me spread the word and I would be most appreciative if you would consider posting your honest thoughts about this book on Amazon.

Your review remains one of the most valuable promotional tools available. Reviews are vital in helping new readers find books they will enjoy reading. So if you've enjoyed this book, please consider leaving an honest rating or review by going to this book's page on Amazon. Good ratings and reviews from readers can help me attract new readers who will also enjoy my writing.

Thank you for your support,

Grace

About the Author

Grace is a well-known parenting author who has written several books on the topic. She has dedicated her life to assisting families through her writings. Her greatest enjoyment in life is being a mother because it's the most gratifying job she's ever had. She likes to write books that touch on all the different aspects of parenting and personal experiences, such as her encounters with her children.

Her love for writing began when she discovered a parenting technique for her explosive son, who was diagnosed with ADHD and ODD, that outperformed others. She was determined to get the word out to other parents as soon as possible. With time, this has developed into something bigger where she is able to share great pieces of advice that can truly change lives.

She also incorporates insights from other parents to offer an enlightening reading experience for all of her readers. Grace hopes that families will be inspired to change the way they think and make better parenting decisions by reading her books.

She enjoys reading novels and watching movies with her family on the weekends.

Visit her profile on Amazon to learn more about her other works - **https://www.amazon.com/author/gracecohen**

Bibliography

Ainsworth, M.D. (December 1969). "Object relations, dependency, and attachment: a theoretical review of the infant-mother relationship". Child Development. 40 (4): 969–1025. doi:10.2307/1127008. JSTOR 1127008. PMID 5360395.

American Academy of Child and Adolescent Psychiatry. (n.d.). Screen Time and Children. Retrieved October 3, 2021, from https://www.aacap.org/AACAP/Families_and_Yout h/Facts_for_Families/FFF-Guide/Children-And-Wa tching-TV-054.aspx.

American Psychological Association. (n.d.). APA Dictionary of Psychology. American Psychological Association. Retrieved October 1, 2021, from https://dictionary.apa.org/will.

American Psychological Association. (n.d.). APA Dictionary of Psychology. American Psychological

Association. Retrieved October 1, 2021, from https://dictionary.apa.org/personality.

American Psychiatric Association, ed. (2013). "Autism Spectrum Disorder, 299.00 (F84.0)". Diagnostic and Statistical Manual of Mental Disorders. Fifth Edition. American Psychiatric Publishing. pp. 50–59.

Bandura A. Toward a Psychology of Human Agency. Perspectives on Psychological Science. 2006;1(2):164-180.

Bandura, A. (1963). Social learning and personality development. New York: Holt, Rinehart, and Winston.

Bi, X., Yang, Y., Li, H., Wang, M., Zhang, W., Deater-deckard, K. (2018). Parenting Styles and Parent-Adolescent Relationships: The Mediating Roles of Behavioral Autonomy and Parental Authority. Front Psychol. 2018;9:2187.

Bretherton, I. (1992). "The Origins of Attachment Theory: John Bowlby and Mary Ainsworth". Developmental Psychology. 28 (5): 759–775.

Castro, V. L., Halberstadt, A. G., Lozada, F. T., & Craig, A. B. (2015). Parents' Emotion-Related Beliefs, Behaviors, and Skills Predict Children's Recognition of Emotion. Infant and child development. 24(1), 1–22.

Centers for Disease Control and Prevention. (25 September 2020). Data & statistics on autism spectrum disorder. Centers for Disease Control and Prevention. Retrieved October 2, 2021, from https://www.cdc.gov/ncbddd/autism/data.html.

Centers for Disease Control and Prevention. (23 September 2021). Data and statistics about ADHD. Centers for Disease Control and Prevention. Retrieved October 2, 2021, from https://www.cdc.gov/ncbddd/adhd/data.html.

Center for Disease Control and Prevention. (6 January 2016). Facts About ADHD. Centers for Disease Control and Prevention. Archived from the original on 22 March 2016. Retrieved October 2, 2021.

Corsello, C., Hus, V., Pickles, A., Risi, S., Cook, E.H., Leventhal, B.L., Lord, C. (September 2007). "Between a ROC and a hard place: decision making and making decisions about using the SCQ". Journal of Child Psychology and Psychiatry, and Allied Disciplines. 48 (9): 932–40. doi:10.1111/j.1469-7610.2007.01762.x. hdl:2027.42/74877. PMID 17714378.

Dobie, C. (2012). "Diagnosis and management of attention deficit hyperactivity disorder in primary care for school-age children and adolescents". p. 79. Archived from the original on March 1, 2013. Retrieved October 2, 2021

Ekman, P. (2005). Basic Emotions. Handbook of Cognition and Emotion. 2005:45-60. doi:10.1002/0470013494.ch3

Harper, D. (n.d.) "empathy". Online Etymology Dictionary.

Hockenbury, D. and Hockenbury, S.E. (2007). Discovering Psychology. New York: Worth Publishers.

Lantz, S.E., Ray, S. (2021). Freud Developmental Theory. [Updated 2021 Feb 7]. In: StatPearls [Internet]. Treasure Island (FL): StatPearls Publishing; 2021 Jan-. Available from: https://www.ncbi.nlm.nih.gov/books/NBK557526/

Merriam-Webster. (n.d.). Will. Merriam-Webster. Retrieved October 1, 2021, from https://www.merriam-webster.com/dictionary/will.

Travel Nunavut. (n.d.). Nunavut fishing traditions. Retrieved October 2, 2021, from https://travelnunavut.ca/things-to-see-do/fishing/nunavut-fishing-traditions/.

Rogers, K., Dziobek, I., Hassenstab, J., Wolf, O.T., Convit, A. (April 2007). "Who cares? Revisiting empathy in Asperger syndrome" (PDF). Journal of Autism and Developmental Disorders. 37 (4): 709–15. doi:10.1007/s10803-006-0197-8. PMID

16906462. S2CID 13999363. Archived (PDF) from the original on October 2, 2021.

Rothbart, M.K. & Hwang, J. (2005). Temperament and the development of competence and motivation. In A.J. Elliot & A.C. Dweck (Eds.). Handbook of competence and motivation. New York: Guilford Press. pp. 167–184. ISBN 978-1-59385-606-9.

Skinner, BF. (1976). About Behaviorism. New York: Random House, Inc. p. 18. ISBN 978-0-394-71618-3.

Silver, L.B. (2004). Attention-deficit/hyperactivity disorder (3rd ed.). American Psychiatric Publishing. pp. 4–7. ISBN 978-1-58562-131-6.

Smith, B.J., Barkley, R.A., Shapiro, C.J. (2007). "Attention-Deficit/Hyperactivity Disorder". In Mash EJ, Barkley RA (eds.). Assessment of Childhood Disorders (4th ed.). New York, NY: Guilford Press. pp. 53–131. ISBN 978-1-59385-493-5.

Werling, D.M., Brand. H., An, J.Y., Stone, M.R., Zhu, L., Glessner, J.T. et al. (April 2018). "An analytical framework for whole genome sequence association studies and its implications for autism spectrum disorder". Nature Genetics. 50 (5): 727–736. doi:10.1038/s41588-018-0107-y. PMC 5961723. PMID 29700473.

Made in United States
North Haven, CT
11 September 2024

57247806R00104